CW00956949

THE CHARACTERISTICS O. ~~~~~~ ~~

A CHARTER FOR IRISH JESUIT COLLEGES

*Jesuit education
intends the full growth of every student,
leading to creative action
that radiates the spirit and presence of Jesus Christ,
the Man for Others.*[1]

EDITED BY BRIAN GROGAN SJ

First published in 2015 by Jesuits in Ireland

Jesuits in Ireland,
Provincial Office, Milltown Park, Dublin 6, Ireland
www.jesuits.ie

Printed in Ireland

ISBN 978-09931675-0-8

Published by Jesuits in Ireland
Designed by Messenger Publications Design Department
Printed by W&G Bairds Ltd

DEDICATION

*This book is dedicated to our staff members, both past
and present, whose personal and professional witness reveals
the best traditions of Jesuit education.*

*It is also dedicated to incoming staff. May it introduce them
to the Jesuit 'way of proceeding' and fire them with
a passion for developing the minds, hearts and souls
of the young men and women entrusted to them.*

ACKNOWLEDGEMENTS

THIS PUBLICATION is the work of many contributors, and to them I owe a great debt of gratitude.

My thanks, above all, go to Fr Brian Grogan, who enthusiastically embraced this project from the outset; what began as a casual conversation became a mission. My hope was to publish a book that would explore, in a clear and direct manner, the spiritual basis for the Jesuit approach to education. I wanted a text that would confidently explain the tradition, but do so in a manner that was sensitive to the concerns and challenges of our times; a text that spoke of things spiritual but was alert to the reality that many people struggle with spirituality and are quickly turned off by clichés. Brian has responded to my invitation by writing a series of reflections that are both wise and eloquent. They come from a lifetime dedicated to living the Jesuit way and to searching for means of communicating it clearly. I am grateful not only for his wonderful insights but also for the accessible and engaging manner in which he has chosen to impart them to us. Brian also acted as editor-in-chief and ensured that deadlines were met and momentum maintained.

Thanks also go to the teachers in our schools who wrote of their own experience of the characteristics as they impacted and inspired their practice. The intention was that Brian's reflections would be complemented by the lived experience of staffs who try on a daily basis to live up to the ideals of Jesuit education. Their accounts are from classroom, playing field, social outreach and the teeming activity that makes up school life. Most of all their accounts are from the heart. They reveal people deeply committed to their profession and fired by the ideal of 'helping souls'. It is clear that they have taken the tradition, made it their own and ensured that it can be passed on intact to the next generation of teachers.

I also thank Deirdre Soffe for her significant contribution to this project. She very kindly interviewed many people in the colleges who were too busy to write up their own accounts but who were keen to make their contributions. Deirdre interviewed twenty-five people in all. She has faithfully recorded their experiences and registered their unique understanding of Jesuit education.

Thanks to Liz Lock, Assistant Editor of *The Way*, for her expertise and unique capacity to track down obscure references; to Phyllis Brady, Jim Culliton SJ, and Mary Murphy for their help at various stages of the project; to Cecilia West of Messenger Publications for her unfailing support for the project and to Paula Nolan for her typical flair with layout and presentation. And finally a word of sincere appreciation goes to Ruth Douglas who coordinated the efforts of all involved with good-humoured aplomb.

Brian Flannery
Delegate for Education in the Irish Jesuit Province

FOREWORD

When the early Jesuits first expressed in a systematic way the concept of Jesuit education, the resulting manual was named the *Ratio Studiorum*. Almost four hundred years later, in 1987, this was updated and named *The Characteristics of Jesuit Education*. It gives expression to what is unique about our educational tradition and is accepted as describing the mission for Jesuit schools worldwide. It is the authoritative statement of 'our way of proceeding' in education.

For many years the Irish Province has relied not only on this lengthy— and sometimes rather dense—statement but also on an excellent summary by Bruce Bradley SJ. His interpretation of the characteristics form the basis for *Jesuit Education—A Charter for the Irish Province* (2011). This has become our mission statement; it is where we look for our inspiration, direction and manner of operation.

The characteristics are therefore at the core of the educational apostolate. Whatever enables them to be better understood and more widely practised is welcome. Hence my pleasure in commending this book to all involved in the schools and colleges.

The present publication is an attempt to reflect on the individual characteristics at more length, and to invite the reader into a deeper consideration of their meaning and relevance for Jesuit schools in Ireland. It aspires to help people really savour the meaning of each of the nine characteristics and to illustrate them in the various accounts from teachers. The book also links the practice in our schools with the spirituality of St Ignatius.

I thank the delegate, Mr Brian Flannery, for initiating this project and seeing it to completion. The more we can become conscious of 'our way of proceeding' the stronger our roots will be and the better prepared for the future we will find ourselves. I thank Fr Brian Grogan for his insightful reflections, and the teachers, not only for their contributions but also for their daily commitment in the service of these worthy ideals.

My hope is that our educational tradition in Ireland may continue to thrive and that the Jesuit project, started so many centuries ago, will continue to respond to the deepest desires of the human heart and the wide-eyed wonder of the blossoming mind.

Fr Tom Layden SJ
Irish Jesuit Provincial

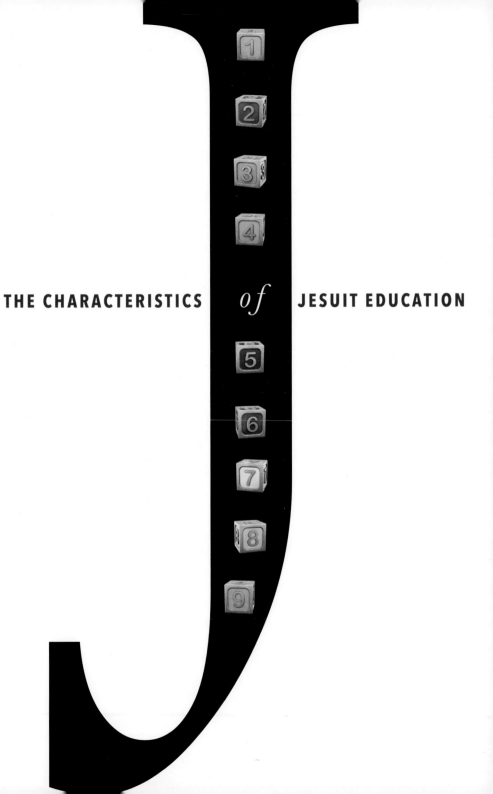

THE CHARACTERISTICS *of* JESUIT EDUCATION

CONTENTS

PREFACE

THIS BOOK, as Fr Provincial says, is about the Jesuit 'way of proceeding' in schools. The focus is on the *character* of a Jesuit education, its values and its world-view. In educational parlance this is more commonly referred to as the 'characteristic spirit' or 'ethos' of a school.

Before considering the special quality or ethos of a Jesuit education I wish to reflect on its purpose; to consider to what end or ends a Jesuit education is directed. In answering the 'what for' question I hope the 'how' of its achievement may be more clearly understood. One informs the other.

A sixteenth-century Jesuit, Diego de Ledesma, succinctly summarised the many fruits of the colleges of his day. Although his comments are somewhat archaic in their expression they are as relevant for today as they were when the schools were first established.

Ledesma saw the Colleges as fulfilling four main purposes. I will comment briefly on each below.

First, they supply people with many advantages for practical living;

secondly, they contribute to the right government of public affairs and to the proper making of laws;

thirdly, they give ornament, splendour and perfection to our rational nature, and

fourth, in what is most important, they are the bulwark of religion and guide us most surely and easily to the achievement of our last end.[2]

"They supply people with many advantages for practical living."
All schools share in this goal. The aim is the full development of the person so that the young man or woman is equipped personally, socially, physically, spiritually and intellectually for adult life and the world of work. Different traditions, however, often place an emphasis that is peculiarly their own; this is to say that in fulfilling this general ambition they impart a certain quality and colour that is distinctive. For the Jesuits the goal of schools has been to cultivate the intellectual talents of the individual and to bring them to the highest point of perfection. Learning is seen as a civilising activity, and so the concern is not simply with intellect and knowledge – although both are good in themselves and essential – but with the development of *pietas*, or character. What is valued most in a mature person is good judgement and good living. This emphasis on intellect, on being the best one can be, and on the importance of reflection is perhaps best summarised by the Jesuit Superior General's call to all of us in the Jesuit tradition to be people of 'depth'.[3] The best preparation for life is to be armed with a keen intellect, strong powers of discernment and an internal moral compass.

"They contribute to the right government of public affairs and to the proper making of laws."
At first the Jesuits were not involved in schools. It was only when the nobility saw the quality of the education that young Jesuits were receiving that they requested the same opportunity be made available to their own children and those of their subjects. Very quickly the Jesuits came to realise the extraordinary potential the schools afforded and they readily embraced the humanist ideal of forming good citizens. Juan de Polanco, secretary to Ignatius, added: 'From among those who are at present only students various persons will in time emerge – some for preaching and the care of souls, others for the government of the land and the administration of justice, and others for other responsibilities. In short, since young people turn into adults, their good formation in life and learning will benefit many others'.[4]

This tradition continues in our schools to this day. Students are taught to be generous in their dealings with one another and to be aware of their responsibilities to the world at large, especially the poor. They are prepared to: 'use their skills of self-expression and advocacy for those who may have no voice' and 'be the agents of change, not more or less passive upholders of the *status quo*'.[5]

Education is about nation-building, and Jesuit schools have been the nurseries of social and political leadership for centuries. The record is not blameless, of course, but many former pupils have served selflessly and successfully. Promoting civic involvement and a global perspective are hallmarks of a Jesuit education.

"They give ornament, splendour and perfection to our rational nature."

This beautiful sentence captures the liberal nature of Jesuit education. Education is not tied simply to economic demands or practical realities but primarily to the full development and flowering of human beings in all their glory. Learning and literacy are seen as good in and of themselves. The emphasis on music, drama, games, debating *et cetera* aims to develop the multiple and diverse talents of the individual. Crucially, these things give pleasure and joy, and reveal the human being's capacity for beauty – the 'ornament and splendour' spoken of by Ledesma. These activities are integral to the civilising influence of schools.

"They are the bulwark of religion and guide us most surely and easily to the achievement of our last end."

Education is not simply about citizenship, although that is clearly a very important consideration. It is also about preparing young people to deal with life's challenging questions and to be attuned to the deeper realities of their own existence. These are philosophical and theological concerns that go to the heart of what life is all about. Throughout a student's time in a Jesuit school the aim is to stimulate and respond in truth and honesty to the spiritual quest in which every thoughtful person will inevitably engage.

The Jesuits propose the Gospel and the Christian tradition as providing rich responses to such questions as to how we should live our lives, relate to our neighbour and deal with adversity and suffering, death and loss. Jesus Christ is seen as the model for human life and the ultimate cause for hope in the face of all our fears and challenges. The hope is that students can be brought to friendship with God and to a sense of the 'sweetness, joy and contentment of things of the spirit' as the Jesuit historian John O'Malley says.[6]

These, then, in summary form, are the noble and ambitious ends that Jesuit education aspires to fulfil. The implicit vision of the human being is grand; the individual is seen in his or her own right, then as intimately related to community and the larger world, and ultimately as somebody who enjoys an eternal destiny. Education is in the service of this ideal – never fully realising it of course but always in pursuit. Our schools are not perfect. But as Ledesma did for his readers nearly five hundred years ago, we present these characteristics as mirroring what we intend. Each graduate expresses the characteristics in his or her own unique way.

And so, having very briefly considered the four general aims of a Jesuit education, I turn to the manner in which they are to be achieved and the reasons for publishing this book. In my role as delegate I often come across teachers and parents who want to know more about the characteristics of Jesuit Education and how these core values relate to everyday practice in the schools. There is a genuine interest in learning about the spiritual and theological perspectives behind the characteristics and in understanding how these are made real and life-giving on a daily basis in the schools.

I think this curiosity arises for two reasons. First, people appreciate that there is something special about what happens in a Jesuit school. Perhaps it is a function of the rich quality of relationships that exist, or the sense of community, or a feeling of purposefulness in all that happens. Whatever it is there is a desire to name it, to put one's finger on what exactly it is, to say 'this is the character of a Jesuit school!'

The second reason relates to a deeper and more elusive point – the existence of a spiritual curiosity or quest that is inherent in all human beings. The dramatic loss of confidence in the Church in recent times and the growing distrust of all things religious make discussion about God and matters of the Spirit very difficult. It is not easy to find a place where this exploration can happen in a meaningful way and a safe environment.

Yet the reality in Ireland is that so much of our culture is still deeply rooted in the Christian tradition and so many of our schools still draw their inspiration from spiritual sources. Despite all the public odium that religion attracts, the fact remains that Catholic schools are still popular and Jesuit schools are all over-subscribed. Something happens in the schools that continues to be valid and valuable, and parents and teachers alike are drawn to it. But they come, as they should, with questions, with a robust critique and a desire for an honest account. This book is an attempt to provide just that.

Whilst some parents may be attracted at first by the 'fruits' of what the tradition offers – the high standards, the breadth and depth of the curriculum, the warm and nurturing relationships, and so on – they may also be touched by an unspoken spirit that breathes through everything that happens. Over time, and as they watch their sons and daughters mature and strengthen, they gain some inkling of what inspires it.

This book is intended to express clearly what is often elusive or left unsaid, and confidently to reconnect the educational tradition with the spiritual insights of Ignatius. It does this while remaining conscious of the individual struggles of faith that people experience and the complexity of modern Irish life. Both Brian Grogan's reflections and the accounts of the teachers are attempts to speak to the spiritual dimension of our being and testify to the continued relevance and vitality of this 'way of proceeding'.

Brian Flannery

Delegate for Education in the Irish Jesuit Province

INTRODUCTION

THESE PAGES describe what Jesuits call 'our way of proceeding' in regard to education. By this is meant the inspiration, values, attitudes and style that have characterised Jesuit schooling for more than 450 years, and which, more importantly, will be found in any truly Jesuit school today. Jesuit education in 2014 is a vast enterprise, involving over 1.6 million students in 2,129 educational institutions across the world. There are only 1,277 Jesuit teachers, while lay persons (along with a small number of religious other than Jesuits) number more than 63,000.[7] The proportion of Jesuits to lay teachers is therefore close to 1:50. This statistic reveals the essentially collaborative nature of Jesuit education today and illustrates the profound contribution that lay teachers make to this joint enterprise. It also highlights the need for Jesuits to share their educational values with lay people, so that the latter may carry forward the authentic Jesuit tradition into the future: hence the present work.[8]

IDENTITY

A Jesuit school or college should be easily identifiable as such. Those involved with it share a common grasp of the educational vision of St Ignatius of Loyola (1491-1556), who was a layman for most of his life, and whose spirituality was forged when he himself was a student, travelling the dusty roads of Europe on foot in search of sound teaching and teaching methods which would be helpful to others.

In a Jesuit school a distinctive spirit lies behind the pedagogy, curriculum and school life, however widely this spirit is adapted to particular times and situations. The description of this spirit given here is intended for Jesuits and lay staff working in Jesuit schools, and also for boards of management, parents, pupils and alumni. This is a working document, not a final statement. Its intention is to encourage critical discussion by presenting the background material – psychological, Ignatian, theological – that underpins the Jesuit educational tradition. The hope is that through dialogue, challenge

17

and mutual enrichment the various stakeholders in a school may draw inspiration and courage from these pages as they labour to renew the Ignatian tradition and so authentically serve the central goals of education in an ever-changing world.

The *credo* of Jesuit education is that God's project in our world is to bring people to the full measure of their humanity. We are to become nothing less than the sons and daughters of God (John 1:12). An early Church writer expresses this tradition magnificently: 'The glory of God is the human person fully alive. The life of the human person is the vision of God.'[9] The project of Jesuit education, then, is to be in tune with God's shaping of the persons committed to our care. We ask: *what would God want for these individuals so that they can freely become what God dreams for them*?

We know something of God's dreams. The New Testament revelation is that there are three persons in the one God. This means that interpersonal relationships are at the core of all reality. Further, this means that right human living is centrally about good relationships – with those around us, with ourselves, and with God. We are born into a world of human relationships – family, friends, fellow students. We come to know ourselves through relating with others: every relationship can be a learning experience, revealing us to ourselves. As we grow in our relations we begin to develop a relationship with the God who has been relating to us all the time. If things go well we become persons who are 'fully alive'.

Human beings develop through reflecting on experience, whether positive or negative, constructive or destructive. This is why reflection is strongly emphasised in our educational system, as will emerge in the course of these pages. In Plato's thought, the unexamined life is not worth living: it is reflection on the stream of our experiences that makes us human.[10] Ignatius asks that whatever may get squeezed out in a busy life, reflection on the day's events, whether good or bad, must remain: otherwise we live in an inner fog and do not know where we are going, nor do we catch the richness hidden in all experiences.[11] TS Eliot speaks of having the experience but missing the meaning, and adds the comforting line, 'Approach to the meaning restores the experience/in a different form, beyond any meaning/we can assign to happiness.'[12]

So we honour students' experience as they move from one level to another. We start from where they are, rather than imposing either human knowledge or Christian faith on them. We hold that if pupils can follow through on their capacity to know the truth and live it out in a loving way, they will become the kind of persons that God wishes them to be. *Men and women for and with others* summarises what we are about. This phrase adapts and develops the ideas of Pedro Arrupe, Superior General of the Jesuits after Vatican II.[13] It emerges from the insight that, since God is a community of Father, Son and Spirit, God wants us to participate as fully as we can in the development of community. This is our project in education: it is nothing less than the co-creation with God of an open universe of relationships.[14]

CONTEMPORARY CULTURE

In Ignatius' day the basic elements of faith could be presumed. These included belief in God and in the need for salvation though Jesus Christ, participation in the prayer and worship of the Christian community, adherence to the moral teaching of the New Testament, aspiration towards the making of a better world. Such cornerstones cannot be presumed today. Jesuit schools are not immune to the prevailing culture of doubt. There are varying levels of belief among pupils and teaching staff, and the Jesuit tradition respects this reality. Prior formation or pre-evangelisation may be required to make pupils aware of the presence of mystery behind human experience. It is within this context that awareness can emerge of the divine Mystery that encompasses human existence. By *mystery* here is meant that which underpins our existence and gives adequate meaning to life. It is too close and pervasive for us to objectify, but we know something about it, whether we name it *God* or not. We are mysteries to ourselves in our origin and our future. Each student is entrusted to us for a brief time, but these interactions are meant to forward the *mystery* of the comprehensive plan of God for all and each of us (see Ephesians 3:5). Thus, while these pages present

Jesuit values as transparently as possible, we acknowledge that we are stewards of a mystery of which we grasp only the outline.

Sceptics may dismiss religious belief as inherently irrational and anti-intellectual. But the tradition of Catholic education respects reason as fully as it respects faith.[15] Those who dismiss as centres of indoctrination schools that have a religious ethos are missing out on the long and rich contribution of Catholic schools to human culture. They miss too the rich diversity within the Catholic sector and the culturally sensitive principles that underpin such education today. The value placed on reason as well as faith helps to explain why Catholic schools are highly popular and respected throughout the world. Catholic education is not self-absorbed but open to the wonder of the ever-expanding universe. The Jesuit tradition shows that it is possible for the same person to be both a rigorous scientist and a sincere believer – witness the life of Pierre Teilhard de Chardin, among many others. God can be found in all things that engage the human mind. Neither reason nor faith need be reduced to accommodate the other. Instead, both play a dynamic role in educating a young person to maturity.

We foster religious literacy in our students. Our alumni, in so far as they are living out their Christian faith, should be able to explain coherently why they believe as they do. They are also to be open to hearing and respecting arguments that oppose their personal beliefs. We understand Christian faith as a reasonable choice that sheds light on the reality of human history. The comment that faith is a leap into the *dark* can be unhelpful. It is rather the lighting of a lantern to pick one's way forward. In the words of Pope Francis: 'Those who believe, see. They see with a light that illumines their entire journey … The light of faith is unique, since it is capable of illuminating every aspect of human existence … Faith does not dwell in shadow and gloom; it is a light for our darkness … a luminous vision of existence … It illumines our human experience from within.'[16] Faith can illuminate contemporary culture, rather than inhibit its development: faith opens windows out on a wider world, and gives meaning to the mystery of human existence.

A WORD ON IGNATIUS

The Jesuit Order was founded by St Ignatius of Loyola, and some knowledge of his remarkable life can be helpful in coming to understand the characteristics of Jesuit education. He came from the Basque region of Northern Spain. His early life offered little prospect of better things to come. He was a wastrel, a brawler, a womaniser. But he was also determined and brave, and as a gentleman-at-arms he led the futile defence of a fortress in Pamplona against the French army in 1521. He was badly injured, after which the defence collapsed. Brought back to Loyola, he endured a long and boring convalescence. The only diversions available were two pious books, a *Life of Christ* and *Lives of the Saints*. These, however, captured his vivid imagination. He slowly learnt to notice the promptings of God, abandoned his past dreams, and gave himself over to the project of Jesus for the salvation of the world.

He became a pilgrim, limping along the roads of Europe and educating himself so that he could serve other people in spiritual affairs. He wanted only 'to help people' for the rest of his life. He began to compose a little volume of exercises for the human spirit, which he built up from personal experience and reading. Full of psychological and spiritual insight, the *Spiritual Exercises* is a small book, which was to change the world.[17] It has been reproduced in some 5,000 editions in a variety of languages. Ignatius also gathered companions bound by a common desire to serve the Church and the world. This culminated in the founding of the Society of Jesus – the Jesuit Order – in 1540. He spent the last sixteen years of his life in Rome administering an ever-growing band of followers. They numbered 1,000 by the time he died. He had not intended to become formally involved in education, but was persuaded in 1547 to open a college in Messina in Sicily. Because of the vision and methods of education that he and his companions elaborated, Jesuit colleges began to appear wherever there were Jesuits to staff them. At the time of his death, there were already 74 colleges on three continents. As an administrator, Ignatius wrote over 7,000 letters; he was also a mystic who lived intimately in the presence of the Trinity. Ignatius is recognised as a man who left his mark on the world and continues to do so through the spread both of the Order and of Ignatian spirituality.

A man of his time, Ignatius met God in many of the ways that we do. God however also chose to encounter him in more dramatic fashion. He experienced profound illuminations, which gave him a deep understanding of what God is about in this world. This was the genesis of his unfettered view of human affairs. God, he believed, can be sought for and found in all things, because God orchestrates *everything* in the service of the divine project for humankind. His hugely influential *Spiritual Exercises* enable people to become available for God's service.

Although a highly capable administrator, he was convinced that the Society of Jesus was not instituted by human means.[18] God, he said, taught him like a school-master, 'perhaps because of his ignorance and obtuse mind'.[19] He understood this as an experience of the divine *cura personalis*. For him the characteristics of Jesuit education are not merely human constructs, but emerge organically from his sense of what God had taught him and how God relates to the human person. In his mind-set, theology and pedagogy are inseparably interwoven: the characteristics mirror his theological convictions. Hence their theological flavour, for the task of sketching the spirituality behind them can be adequately achieved only by constant reference to the theology that underpins all Ignatian spirituality.[20]

We shall say more about Ignatius later in dealing with the ideal of greater service.[21] It is time now to elaborate the characteristics of Jesuit education.

SEARCHING FOR TRUTH ... AND FINDING GOD

EXPERIENCE

Ignatius had an uncomplicated ideal: he simply wanted 'to help people' and had an uncanny gift for being able to do so. He accepted people where they were on their life-journey and assisted them to take their next feasible step forward. So we, too, start with pupils as they present themselves, and we respect their experience. James Joyce's Stephen Dedalus took this to heart, even though it brought him to conclusions unintended by his Jesuit teachers: 'Welcome, O life! I go to encounter for the millionth time *the reality of experience* and to forge in the smithy of my soul the uncreated conscience of my race.'[22]

Fundamentally pupils come as learners. They have 'the pure desire to know'.[23] They are hungry for knowledge. But the search for truth is well under way before they enrol with us. We help them to continue it through all the subjects in which they engage. Ours is not a 'drainpipe model' of learning, which presumes an empty student mind needing to be filled. 'Education' comes from the Latin *e-ducere*, meaning 'to draw out'. So we try to draw out what is within the pupils – here, the potential hidden in their experience. We also offer students a *liberal* education, an approach to learning that empowers and prepares them to deal with complexity and change: 'A liberal education helps students develop a sense of social responsibility, as well as strong and transferable intellectual and practical skills such as communication,

:ical and problem-solving skills, and a demonstrated ability to knowledge and skills in real-world settings.'[24]

Incoming students have already picked up parental values, insights, beliefs, prejudices and limits. The spectrum of their backgrounds is wide. For some, because of family practice, religious belief may have come easily and unnoticed. For others, the opposite may be the case. What they all have in common, however, according to Aristotle long ago, is the desire for happiness.[25] Jesuit education promotes this desire by cultivating student imaginations and developing their sensitivity to all that is human – relationships, friendships, love, but also failure and suffering, which can open doors to the deeper questions. Nothing human is alien to Jesuit education. Hence much has been written about Ignatian humanism, which respects all creation, defends all that is good in human affairs, and sees God as everywhere active in the world.[26] Through exploring the human, the divine emerges, for what makes us more human makes us more like God. The road to God is through the human heart.

THE CHALLENGE TO BELIEVE

Does belief matter? We say that it does, that it is intrinsic to full human development; so we offer a framework in which finding God becomes a value. In 1977 Kenneth Galbraith wrote *The Age of Uncertainty*, documenting the impact of economic history on social and political life and thought.[27] The age of uncertainty that he described is still with us. Agnosticism, secular humanism, atheism, uncertainty and indifference are attractive in our times. Belief in God was easy for Ignatius in the sixteenth century, but today the very mention of God, much less of what Ignatius called 'finding God in all things' can be disconcerting.[28] And so, the better place to begin a faith journey is by searching for authenticity. Inauthentic living can be characterised by self-centredness, over-emphasis on the rational to the exclusion of the heart and affectivity, and the narrowing of hope to intra-worldly horizons. Authentic living means that one is open to follow the pure desire to know, without ever setting limits to the quest for intelligibility and the inner urge to live according to the truth.

24

Thus, while we foster academic excellence, we focus on a wider horizon, beyond particular items of knowledge and particular skills and interests. Even at a young age, children see human living and the world in a certain way. They have an incipient philosophy of life. We build on that philosophy, question it, challenge and develop it. We help students to explore the deeper questions as these arise for them through what they read, see and hear, and through their engagement with life. We encourage their commitment to truth, wherever it leads. Ultimately it will lead into Mystery. For mystery is not far from each of us. Each of us is a mystery: we don't understand ourselves. Each human being is wonderful, awesome. Those who fall in love catch on to the mystery that is the other. Experience and observation of life – of global or personal tragedies, political unrest, war, inequality, poverty – bring the deeper questions into consciousness. We could ignore these realities in favour of purely academic knowledge, but we don't. We prompt and support the student's search for meaning in them.

So, through teaching, conversation, relationship, reading and debate, we invite reflection on the issues of ultimate importance. What is life about? What are we meant to be? Am I worthwhile? Are we going anywhere? What does a worthwhile life look like? How can I make a difference? What sort of difference do I want to make? What would promote justice, peace, fair distribution of wealth, safety of the environment and world peace? Do I care whether others are happy so long as I am?

Through the habit of making well-informed choices a spirituality of searching and finding emerges, as does the development of a contemplative attitude. Contemplation has been described as taking a long, loving look at things, even those that are distasteful or frightening. This practice can lead to wondering what God might be inviting us to do. Take the image of a pair of scissors. The lower blade symbolises reality as we find it around us. The upper blade symbolises values and the knowledge and skills that come from good education. Our task is to hone the upper blade in order that it can cut through the chaos obscuring the good in our fragile world, so that we can see what we ought to do.

THE CHRISTIAN VISION

The questions that arise from life, from literature and from the world of scientific discovery can lead students towards their own interpretations of life and to wide religious horizons. We Jesuits were once students ourselves: we have asked ourselves the same questions as our students do. Like everyone else, we go through the dark hours of doubt. But we find in Jesus Christ the most satisfying interpretation of human existence, and so we propose it to our students for their consideration. We respect the spectrum of their responses, from enthusiasm through agnosticism to scepticism. In some of our schools the majority of pupils are grounded in Christian values, in others Christians are a small minority. We sow the seeds of transcendence and trust that these will grow to harvest in God's good time.

Christians find it reasonable to believe that God exists; that God makes, sustains and loves the world; and that God is fully on the side of humankind; that God wants the fullness of life for all, since we are made in the divine image and likeness (Genesis 1:28); that God desires our happiness, and that our destiny is to live forever with God and one another in joyous community. God's chosen way of leading us to this goal, we hold, is revealed, unexpectedly but decisively, in the person of Jesus of Nazareth. At once human and divine, he is what we are to become. Our calling is to become the sons and daughters of God (see John 1:12). As CS Lewis observes, in this world, despite appearances, there are no ordinary mortals, only extraordinary immortals.[29]

Further, Christians hold that the Christian community, the Church, despite all its defects, contains in embryo the final community for which we are made. Its foundation is the reality of God as three Persons who live together in harmony and invite us to share their life. The treasure entrusted to the Church for the world is the revelation of God's love for the world and how God is working to reverse the cycle of human decline. Left to ourselves, we humans are incapable of sustained development: evil, sin and death blight the best-intentioned of human enterprises. But God's designs for a world of just and loving relationships are already under way and, to achieve them, God engages us as collaborators. We must not compound the problem by muddling along with our own internally generated recipes for the well-being of the world and of ourselves. We are to be carriers of the divine solution. With God we are to construct a new world order, a civilisation of love.

Such, we believe, is the divine project and our important role in it. We respect alternative views, but we see the Christian perspective on human history as the most comprehensive and satisfying. It is based, not on wishful thinking, but on the historical reality of Jesus of Nazareth: what he did and who he was. Thus the search for truth proposed in the first characteristic brings us forward to 'finding God in all things'. This phrase emerged as Ignatius' statement of how he tried to work with God in the enterprise of bringing love and meaning into a fragmented and dysfunctional world.

FINDING GOD IN ALL THINGS?

The popularity of Ignatian spirituality is constantly growing because people discover in it the answers to their deepest questions. There are stages in this process of finding God, and as pupils mature we offer them further insights. The first stage is when wonder and curiosity lead a student to explore the deeper meaning of life. The next stage is the awareness of the divine project for the world. There then begins a life of relationship with God, and a desire within the student to align his or her life with the divine project, as Jesus did. He could say, 'I do nothing of myself … he who sent me is with me, and has not left me to myself, for I always do what pleases him' (John 8:28-29).

The search for God grows into a rich and unending voyage of discovery. The scope of the adventure is the reality of God, of the created universe and of all human history. Nothing is irrelevant, for God, we claim, is in all. But is this true? Take up your daily paper and ask yourself: can God be found in everything in these pages and columns? In sport, sex, science, space exploration, scandals, crime, births, marriages and deaths? It seems impossible, yet God is Creator and author of all being, so all reality leads to and reveals something of God. The labour of trying to find God is worthwhile and brings happiness. Thomas Merton says, 'The gate of heaven is everywhere'; every discovery leads further into the Great Mystery.[30] We begin to see the world as God sees it, and so everything becomes a signpost to God. A steadiness of purpose encompasses life's unforeseen variables.

FINDING GOD IN THE WORLD

Where to start in the quest for God? It is easy to find God in nature, in its wonder, order and imagination. Nature is God's first self-revelation. God, in Hopkins's phrase, is revealed as 'beauty's self and beauty's giver'.[31] Next, we can begin to interpret the unfolding history of the world as sacred history because God is involved in it. This transforms our watching of the television news! We learn to understand good events as coming from the hand of a caring and provident God, and bad events as the arena for God's transforming labours by which evil becomes the occasion of good. There grows a sense of the divine as the milieu of our lives, as Teilhard de Chardin noted.[32] Further we can develop a simple intimacy and familiarity with God in prayer and life. The freshness of Christ can attract us as it did Ignatius. We come to pray for the world and to care for it deeply. Supported by Ignatius' example, we try 'to keep God always before our eyes' in our decision making. We find ourselves working in partnership *with* a labouring God, rather than playing the 'lone ranger', tackling impossible tasks single-handedly.

GOD'S IMAGES

Moving further, it is exciting to see persons as they are – as images of God. Our relationships become grounded in limitless respect, no matter how odd or difficult the other may appear. As St Paul reminds us, each person is 'a brother for whom Christ died' (1 Corinthians

8:11), so everyone is of infinite value, at least to God's way of thinking. As people-watchers, looking at the crowds in a shopping mall, we can try, like Francis of Assisi, to see there the image of God 'multiplied but not monotonous'.[33] We begin to wonder about others and what their stories may be. We can imagine how God is working to shape them according to the divine dream. Classrooms and crowded corridors take on a new dimension from this perspective. We become minor mystics as we learn to see into the mystery of things. And this is important: the Jesuit theologian Karl Rahner remarked more than thirty years ago that the Christian of the future would have to be a mystic, or would not exist at all. By 'mystic' he meant *someone who has really experienced God*.[34] We have a better chance of helping students to see the divine reality of others if we have a sense that we too are nothing less than 'God's beloved' (see Romans 1:7).

SERVICE

God is labouring indefatigably in the messiness of things (See *Spiritual Exercises*, n.236) and so we are challenged to find what God may want done in the unlovely and chaotic dimensions of life. This demands the alignment of our decisions with God's project. That project clarifies as the building up of good relationships around us. The Ignatian phrase 'in all things love and serve' (*Spiritual Exercises*, n.231) catches the point. I want to put God first and, like Ignatius, to be led by Another.[35]

For busy people, Ignatius proposes the Examen – also called the Examination or Review of Consciousness (*Spiritual Exercises*, nn.32–43) as a daily help by which we rummage through the day that has passed and become more sensitive to where God was present and where we, perhaps, were insensitive to divine invitations. The Review develops in us a grateful heart or God's gracious interventions in the day, and enables us to find God ever more spontaneously. We come to share our lives with God. At meetings we begin to ask: 'what is God's agenda, rather than our own?' What might be the wisest and most caring decision among the various options presented? How can I be a spokesperson for the Gospel values involved? What might God want me to do in the laborious task of implementing decisions?[36] A life of loving service begins to take shape, and this works for the good of the world.

FINDING GOD IN SUFFERING

It is hard to find God in the negative aspects of life. We may not even want to try since we tend to avoid what makes us uncomfortable. But students want to know how, if God exists and is good, suffering and evil can also exist. Belief in God is easily eclipsed by natural and human tragedies. To draw meaning out of evil and suffering is indeed hard work. But we can help our pupils to search for God hidden in the world's tears, and to notice that God is always working to bring good out of what is bad. It is not that God undoes the hurt and restores the previous *status quo*, but that God provides help that enables the sufferer to cope. From the death of Jesus we learn what Christian tradition calls 'the dynamic of the Cross' – namely that unavoidable suffering, patiently endured, becomes a blessing for the sufferer and for the world. This is the critical insight gained from watching with the eyes of faith what occurred on Calvary, and how in Christian understanding '*bad* Friday' became '*good* Friday'. We come to believe that God is not distanced from pain but is in solidarity with those in misery. We learn to pray for the world in its grief, and we ask to be shown what role we can play in alleviating the anguish of others. 'What ought I to do for Christ and for his suffering brothers and sisters?' (See *Spiritual Exercises*, n.53.)

When problems are humanly insoluble, faith edges us towards belief in the life of the world to come. The radical healing by God of the ravages of suffering, evil and death occurs not within this world but in the Great Fulfilment, when all is made new (see Revelation 21:5). God's preferred mode of operating is not to wipe out these dark realities but to *integrate* them into the eternal weave. While sorrow remains part of human life, and evil a dark mystery, faith offers us enough light to remain firm in the belief that God cares. We notice with wonder that God continues to respect human freedom, even at its worst. We catch on to the mystery whereby evil becomes the occasion of great good, and how pain can be the occasion of bringing to birth unimagined levels of love and forgiveness.

Giving time to noticing God in the reality of daily living brings deep personal enrichment and also enriches others. And of course it is school life itself that provides us with our primary challenge to find God.

SUMMARY

Jesuit education begins from the living experience of pupils: it is here that God is at work.

Jesuit education is conducted in a spirit of reverence and a commitment to truth, wherever it leads.

Religious belief is reasonable and brings light to the dark dimensions of life.

Ignatian humanism respects all creation, defends all that is good in human affairs and sees God as everywhere active in the world.

Whatever makes us more human makes us more like God. The divine is in our DNA.

The scope of Jesuit education is unrestricted, since God is to be encountered in all things. 'All things' include suffering, evil and death, because God works to integrate them into the divine enterprise of leading us to lasting happiness.

SEARCHING FOR TRUTH ... AND FINDING GOD!

LIVING EXPERIENCE

EXPONENTIAL FUNCTION
Seamus Ahearne

I want to start by looking at a maths scenario, taken from the new Project Maths course. It involves compound interest and looking at the way interest can grow.

So we start with a simple situation in which I invest €100 for one year and I negotiate the amazing interest rate of 100% from my local friendly bank manager. Actually this example will work with any rate, but 100% keeps it very easy to calculate. So now, at the end of the year, I have €200 in my account. In other words, my money has doubled, or has had a multiplier of 2. If I had gone back to the manager and negotiated for the interest to be split and added at the end of each six month period, I would have ended up with €225, or a multiplier of 2.25. Now I'm thinking about getting interest added at the end of each month, and I find out that I would get the amount of €261, or a 2.61 multiplier. So if I were to keep looking for interest to be added at shorter intervals I would find that every week would give me a multiplier of 2.69, every day would give a multiplier of 2.714, every hour 2.7181, every minute 2.7182, and so on. Eventually I would start to see very little deviation from 2.71828162 ...

Now, what is that number and why is it so important?

Well, it is called 'e', and it was first defined by the Swiss mathematician Leonhard Euler in 1748, although the Scottish mathematician John Napier had also referred to it in 1614 when he was developing his work on logarithms. It is now commonly called the Exponential Function, and it describes patterns of growth. So in many different areas where elements are changing rapidly, perhaps in a seemingly chaotic or random way, if we look more closely at how the growth or change is occurring we will see that it is somehow closely related back to 'e' or some function of 'e'.

For instance, if we measure the apparently chaotic spread of bacteria, or the rate at which the rainforests are being depleted, we will find 'e' lurking. If we examine the concept behind nuclear reactors, the nuclear chain reaction, we will find that the rate of fission increases exponentially. If we look at the growth in world population or the rate at which waterlilies spread across a lake, the spread of internet traffic or the rising demand for drinking water, or a whole host of other random scenarios where change is occurring we will undoubtedly find 'e', the Exponential Function.

For me this symbolises the constancy beneath all the seeming chaos. It suggests a pattern underpinning events in nature that seem at times totally random and unplanned. At a deeper level, it suggests to me that, beneath the destructive power of a nuclear explosion, or within the beauty of spreading waterlilies or the alarming growth of a deadly bacteria, there is a constant. There is a connection and a plan and a pattern and bedrock. For me it suggests the hand of God, the meaning that underlies the apparent madness.

Seamus Ahearne is a teacher of maths at Clongowes Wood College SJ.

SEEING GOD'S HAND AT WORK
Gerry J Foley

Since I began working at Belvedere College, I have started to spend more time reflecting on my own experience. For the first time in my professional life as a teacher I have had an opportunity to facilitate my spiritual development. To experience reflective space within an incredibly busy environment has been one of the delights of my time at the College. Students here also have reflective space as part of their educational experience. I have witnessed the process that provides the environment for students to develop a personal spirituality enhanced by their experiences during their time at the school.

The characteristics of Jesuit education lie at the heart of the ethos of a Jesuit School. They form the framework that underpins the whole educational experience of the community. These characteristics have helped form my own understanding of my role as a teacher in a Catholic educational environment. One of the characteristics is that those in the school may come to see God in all things. The invitation to seek and find God in everything has been at the heart of my experience at Belvedere College. The desire is for students to contemplate the world in which they exist and seek an understanding of God's role in it. This can be a very difficult concept for them to grasp at times. In an increasingly secular world, where religion is viewed with scepticism and hostility, there can be a reluctance in some young people to promote their faith. However, by communicating your own unique world-view and personal experience you can inspire and provoke the students to look at their own experiences. This can stir a momentary realisation of God's presence in their lives. Each opportunity to engage in reflection brings about change.

When I engage with the students I do so from a personal perspective on my life and experiences. I cannot separate myself from my personal convictions. I convey my understanding about my world and life experiences so that they can react and respond from their own perspective. This process provides an opportunity for growth, for change and for a deeper understanding of faith. My teaching is driven and promoted by my faith experience, and it is out of this that I hope to inspire my students to know the presence of God in their lives.

The Parable of the Sower comes to mind in explaining how I see my role as a teacher of religious education I sow every day, and have done so through many years of working with young people, and I am not aware of the impact I may have had. The focus for the students at Belvedere College is on taking the time to reflect on their own unique experience. When we pray we stop and think. We contemplate and put our lives into some kind of perspective when seen against the experiences of others in the world. Every day I remind students to consider their situation with gratitude, to understand the fragility of life and to grasp how best to appreciate our existence. When I pray with my students in the classroom, the oratory, the chapel or on retreat, I invite them to think of family, of friends, of encounters in their day; then I try to make the link with God's hand at work. Finding God in all things is about inviting the students to see the world in a way that opposes the anti-God, anti-religion world-view.

The reflective time during the course of a busy day at school is important for both students and teachers. They stop and think. A few moments of silence and stillness at the start of a lesson sheds light on what's important. The use of such resources empowers the students to take a look at life and consider another viewpoint. The weekly Examen is a practice that enhances spiritual, emotional and mental well-being. The opportunity to meditate and relax in a prayerful and comfortable environment provides a very beneficial experience.

I hope that my students have been given a framework that caters for personal reflection and opens their hearts and minds to understanding their relationship with God.

Gerry J Foley is a teacher of religion at Belvedere College SJ.

THE UNDERPINNING VALUES
A conversation with Carmel MacGabhann

Our implementation of the characteristics of Jesuit education is greatly helped by a number of programmes. The school is fortunate to be able to resource a social outreach post, as well as offering retreat opportunities to all of the year groups. All students benefit from this, as there is a strong component of *personal* development built into these experiences, quite apart from the religious elements. Through the Kairos retreat the students facilitate younger students. They reflect on their ordinary life together and they get an enormous amount out of this.

The iconography in the school is important, as you pick up the ethos by osmosis. The induction programme helps new staff as it gives them a chance to hear more about the Jesuit approach to education before they start.

The characteristics are listed in the school journal, and I see the concept of 'finding God in all things' as an individual way of looking at life, a lens that sees the world from a particular angle. The boys have an invitation to look at things this way.

The idea of being a person for others is very attractive to the boys, and it gives them an opportunity to look beyond themselves to contribute to others' well-being. The media focus on exam results is unfortunate, and as Gonzaga does well, some students develop a false sense of entitlement as a result: they feel that they will excel simply by being in the school. The social outreach programme focuses on their obligation to give something back. A wide range of activities is available, and the boys love being involved. I try to make them aware of the application of this principle within the classroom as well. I point out that it is the measure of them if they can contribute when there is no gain for themselves in doing so. You see this in strong students who are taking lower level subjects – they should put in the same effort and behave as they would in any of their other classes. Society at large promotes self-interest, but even in the classroom this can be challenged.

The atmosphere in the college could be described as active and inclusive in regard to religion. Reflection and discussion are fostered. Opposing views are respected. A staff retreat is offered and Mass is available. The fact that the practice of religion is visible in the school makes it easier to discuss with the boys the values underpinning their education.

Carmel MacGabhann is a teacher of Irish at Gonzaga College SJ.

GOD IN ALL THINGS
Mary Maume

When I was asked to make a contribution to this process, I reflected on life here in Clongowes: are we faithful to the Ignatian understanding of trying to find God in all things: the good, the bad and the ugly? I wonder are we taking enough time to teach boys how to stand still and how to take some quality time in the midst of a very busy day to meet God.

We are privileged to be in the heart of the country and from every window there is a view of God's creation in the magnificent colours of nature. How do we help the students encounter God in this beauty that surrounds them, in this oasis of calm in the heart of Kildare?

I was in the midst of the Kairos Retreat preparation at the time of my interview for this piece: that frenetic ten minutes we squeezed in before lunch. I spoke about training nine Rhetoric students to take the lead in this peer ministry retreat. The role of leadership is privileged, as it obliges the leaders firstly to reflect on the most fundamental question: 'who am I,' before they can move on to consider images of God. As eighteen-year-old students, they have to find a language to talk about God to their peers in Poetry: that is challenging and it obliges them to delve a little deeper into their own sense of God.

My fear is that these leaders are trying to explain the God-concept to their peers without having had the reflective space to consider this, because of the huge demands on their lives. Where are they meeting God in their daily occupations? There is a huge desire to find something; there are needs not being met through social media. At one level there is a connection, but is it real? For example, three people in a pub are looking sadly into their pint of beer when a friend texts to enquire how the evening is progressing. The three immediately respond with a picture of three smiling individuals who appear to be having the time of their lives. This image is sent to friends and posted on Facebook. The drinkers may not be feeling too positive about their own lives or their self-image – but the message is that three people are having the most wonderful time drinking beer and that their lives are perfect in every way. This illustrates the superficiality of this world of social media.

The needs of the soul are not being met through the world of social media. Yes, people connect, but at what level? That is the issue. Life is about living and in that living people encounter happiness, sadness and all that occurs in between. The world of appearances does not take account of the inner world of the individual, which also needs to be acknowledged and fed. The speed of life and of the images that hit people's consciousness alienates them from their inner world; in fact, they do not even acknowledge that there is a possibility of an inner world that should be the guiding light in their lives.

I feel that in the past, things moved slower and the person got more time to think, to reflect and to plan for the future. The sense of soul was being fed, even if people were not fully aware of that, because we were obliged to face our emotions: there was nowhere else to go. Today we can live almost parallel lives because of social media. Whether or not people accepted the institutional Church and all it offered, it loomed large in their lives and was a tapestry where soul-searching could occur.

When I discussed this with the Kairos leaders, they agreed that when an issues arises, they immediately air it on Facebook or equivalent, so instead of going inside and meeting the self in stillness, there is the immediate desire to place it outside, hoping to find some resolution. They are less likely to withdraw to a quiet place, although we have three chapels here in Clongowes and a Prayer Room. Our problem is that when we ask them to try and find God in that small quiet space within, it is almost alien to them. Nevertheless the desire to search and to find is very strong and at some level they are aware that their current way of living and being is not meeting the deepest desires of the soul. Life is lived on the surface and in some cases is snuffed out on the same surface.

I think of soul as that great ball of energy, that Eros that is stirring deep within us, that very ingredient that keeps us together especially when we are confronted with the challenges of living in the world, but we have to find a creative way to help young people search for that energy within rather than without. Facebook and social media does not give young people freedom within, as they are constantly needing reassurance from this artificial world that they are good enough, are beautiful enough and 'cool' enough.

As I prepared Morning Prayer recently I quoted from a piece on St Ignatius. It related to slowing down, to listening, to being patient: 'Our ears should be wide open to our neighbours until they seem to have said all that is on their mind.'

I asked the boys to listen and to listen properly, so perhaps creative listening might help to bridge this gap between the outside and the inside. Listening at the level of soul has a sacredness attached to it: you feel you are on another level. It is real and the one being listened to leaves feeling refreshed and connected.

So how do we help them find integration? If we follow in the footsteps of Ignatius, we really have to help people find that reflective spot in themselves and it will ultimately lead to greater internal freedom. We should be spending more time on the Characteristics and on delving deeper into the Exercises to make sense of life for ourselves and those we teach.

Mary Maume is a school counsellor at Clongowes Wood College SJ.

ALLOWING GOD INTO OUR WORLD
Daniel McNelis

'Finding God in ALL things' is a refreshing and enriching challenge for Christians. Its unspoken continuation might be … *not just in Mass, sacraments or other God stuff, but everywhere.* We compartmentalise God: it's about time that we allowed God out into the world, which, after all, he has created. And as we compartmentalise God, we are inclined to do the same with our own lives. We are prone to distinguish between the 'sacred' experience of religious ritual, where God is 'present' and the 'secular' realm of our studying, socialising, playing and family lives, where God is 'absent'. The poet Patrick Kavanagh speaks of a man who 'coughed the prayer phlegm up from his throat' at the end of Sunday Mass for another week.[37] This in many ways sums up an Irish attitude to faith – as something restricted to ritual, rather than an all-consuming loving relationship, which informs and enriches all our day's diversity.

Our lives involve a sequence of human encounters and relationships. Each day we interact in a variety of ways with other people. More intimately put, we live, person to person. Humans seem to need this contact with other humans. As society becomes more individualistic, does it become more isolating? Loneliness is fast becoming a major concern for mental health and personal well-being. It's no surprise that in the penal system, solitary confinement is regarded as an effective punishment and deterrent. We need others to enrich us, to irritate us, to challenge us to become the persons we are destined to be. If this is the key human experience and the kernel of our lives, it is also the realm in which we find God – in the totality of our moment to moment experiences.

While the notion of the universal accessibility of God is attractive and energising, it is also challenging. How do I deal with the person who invariably irritates me, the bore, the one who often criticises me, the needy one whose dependence exhausts me? The visiting Greeks said to Philip, 'We should like to see Jesus' (John 12:21). Would I? Would I really like to see Jesus in those I encounter daily? Do I feel drawn to the biblical call to love my neighbours, not simply to like or tolerate them? Perhaps life was easier when we had God safely 'corked' in the bottled ritual of Masses, funerals and weddings. But let God out and now he invades all our 'secular' space and relationships. Now, not only rites of passage, but 'all things' are sacramentalised and reveal God.

With St Ignatius we pray: '… teach me to be generous, to serve you as you deserve, to give and not to count the cost …' We need this selflessness in order to find God in all things. And, of course, we simply cannot do it without prayer. It's too much for us to achieve on our own. It is far easier for us to ride roughshod over others whenever the mood takes us.

When I was studying abroad, a fellow student, remarking that I was Irish, asked, 'Are you a Christian, then?' Rather smugly I replied that I was. 'And the duty of the Christian is to love others, isn't it?' Less enthusiastically I agreed that such was the case. This gave him the perfect opening. 'Well, I don't believe in any God, so you have to love me, but I don't even have to like you!' he said as he jauntily walked away. I was left seething! This individual was thoroughly obnoxious, inconsiderate and selfish, and universally disliked by his fellow students. Yet, … he was right. I had 'signed up' to love others, enemies specified. The Prayer for Generosity came in handy on that occasion.

Jesuit schools are much sought after owing to their reputation for pedagogical expertise in a well-organised search for knowledge, meaning and truth. Parents and pupils are happy to make a personal investment in and commitment to this. The 'truth' of Jesuit education, however, is ultimately a relationship, founded in a person who claimed to be the embodiment of truth itself: 'I AM the truth' (John 14:6). To seek the truth in learning, and in encounters and activities of all sorts, is to seek to bring into our lives that relationship with the one who IS truth.

What a wonderfully worthwhile endeavour! Suddenly, all activity has added value. The repetitive drudgery of learning or housework, the meaningless commute, the grind of obligation, smiling tolerance of the intolerable person – all are transformed and invested with ultimate meaning. Little, perhaps, do we realise that in our seemingly meaningless daily tasks we have steadily been building the Kingdom of God. We can be enlightened and encouraged by the capacity to find God in the everyday: thereby we find ourselves living lives of real meaning, purpose and joy.

Danny McNelis is a teacher of religion at Gonzaga College SJ.

DO WHAT YOU ARE DOING
A conversation with Padraic O'Sullivan
When you start teaching in a Jesuit school you are looking around you, looking at the way things are done there. I suppose you are really wondering about the culture, and how you will fit in. When I began, I was struck by the staff's deep respect for each student. Standards were high. I saw that teachers tried to capture the imagination and the curiosity of each student.

What influenced me most was the example of other people. I was aware of writings on Jesuit education but these can be too much for a new person to take in. Sometimes you make the mistake of trying to do it all at once, and things do not work that way. This is where the title of my piece came from. There was a wonderful Jesuit with whom I worked, and I admired his approach. His advice was, 'do what you are doing'. It sounds simple, but he encouraged me to give everything to the moment in hand. His own example illustrated the advice. He worked with care, with effort, with attention and with love. Hidden in the simplicity of his message was the encouragement, 'work at your best, for others'.

The Jesuit way of serving others is practical. There is great joy in the gospel, and it is in the joy of life that we find God in all things. One Jesuit took delight in telling me that the Jesuits in California had set up a vineyard: perhaps he hoped to be transferred there!

The possibility of finding God in all things influences the way we approach the educational experience. At a practical level each department's syllabus must be followed and our students want to do well in their exams. However, from the beginning, Ignatius had the view that education was a preparation for life, so the whole person – heart, mind, body and soul – has to be taken into account. There is a unity in what is being done in the school. Assured of God's love, and with an appreciation of God's unique gifts to each, the students develop a mature self-confidence that prepares them for life. Education is also about how we build relationships. People have to be comfortable with themselves and with others. You need a certain freedom of mind to achieve this. Our graduates who grasp this approach are confident and accepting of themselves and others, they have a sense of purpose in what they do. This is confidence at its best – of course misplaced confidence translates into a type of arrogance or elitism, which completely misses the point.

A Jesuit delivering a talk in the school once said, 'If the Jesuits were not in education they would be trying to get into it'.

Padraic O'Sullivan is now retired and taught Latin and Greek at Gonzaga College SJ.

FINDING GOD IN THE HERE AND NOW
A conversation with Michael Sheil SJ

Finding God in all things – it's in the here and now! When we were young Jesuits our Master of Novices warned us against entertaining utopian views of what we would do for Christ in faraway places and on the mission fields. But what about what he called the '*hic*' and '*nunc*' (the 'here' and 'now') with your family, your school, your community? I have always struggled with theory: I am more of an active person. I find it easier to do the thing, rather than develop a theory.

When I think of finding God in all things, I like to turn the notion around, and think that God finds me in whatever it is I do, whether I'm talking to the little fellows, or having the craic with the sixth years. I have had very different roles here: for eighteen years I was the higher line prefect, so I was like the 'chief gaoler'; and then I had suddenly to change into a sort of 'Red Coat' in Butlins holiday camp! I help now with games, with some co-curricular activities and with some prefecting – as well as being Rector in the Jesuit Community.

In doing what we are doing, it's important to remember the search for excellence. Some people misinterpret this. It is an aim, not a claim. We attempt to achieve excellence, and the effort is ongoing, every day, no matter what a boy's level or standard. Clongowes is good at bringing people on: a 'D' student can become a 'C' student. In rugby no one is written off.

I think that being in a boarding school is a great advantage because it enables us to give an example of how we live these ideals. Companionship is what lasts and really influences the boys, and sometimes it is in the down time, when things are not organised, that they really get to make friends. That sense of companionship is present in the other schools, too. When I was chaplain in Belvedere I remember a Rhetoric student saying to me that he never went to bed in bad form on a Sunday night because he knew he would be going into Belvedere the next day. There was a pervasive sense of community.

At the start of each year, when I'm getting to know the new students, when they chat about their families, I often ask about their Confirmation. What difference did it make to them – apart from the financial benefit? Whether it's preparation for First Communion or for Confirmation, the schools try to do a great job, but as things are currently organised the parents are often left on the sidelines. Perhaps too much responsibility is handed over to the schools. The current structure in patronage of the schools may change and perhaps improve the situation. Parishes must try to get involved, but of course that only works if the family is already attending the parish.

The level of knowledge and exposure to faith can vary hugely: for some it's minimal. The fellows are very honest, they'll say that the only time they are faced with the practice of religion and the expression of their faith is in a place like this. Some time ago the Headmaster took the initiative by taking Mass to the Sports Hall. The space there can be configured easily to look like a modern church: some people did not think this was a great idea. However, it has given both boys and parents a richer experience of liturgy. What the Headmaster is trying to do is to speak in a language that can be heard by the boys; but they may be held back by a lack of basic background knowledge of religion – the mystery of God's love in our daily lives – and our response to that Love in our relationships with others.

However, we continue and hope that something will take root. I say Mass here every morning before the bell. In a Jesuit boarding school there should always be the possibility of Mass for anyone who may wish to attend. 'God in all things'!... We should have visible evidence of this each day here, whether Mass is well attended or not. Some will say they are not religious but that they are spiritual. I have heard it said that the spiritual is about 'me', whereas religion is about 'we'. Religion is the expression of my spirituality within community. We are losing that sense of community, and this loss predates the Celtic Tiger.

For the past six or seven years, at Easter I have gone to Lesotho with a group of fifth years and we work with the local community. The fellows are always struck by the sense of community and the happiness of people who, by comparison to us, have absolutely nothing. The phrase 'men and women for others' is one that really catches on. It sums up how we are trying to get them to engage socially. My hope is that what we do there may find a deep-rooted place in their consciousness, that later on in life it may mean something to them. When we are there, we do some reflection, and I hope that that experience helps them always to come back to the 'here-and-now', so that they ask: *how does that experience which I have just had change my life in the present? What is it that speaks to me out of my present experience?*

We are not unique in having *cura personalis* as a core value. What I hope is that students can see in me somebody who cares about them. Even by greeting them in the corridor I can give them a sense that they are important in my life. I'm not just looking after them but making myself available for them. Even if I have a difference of

45

opinion with them, or a matter of discipline, I want them to see that their happiness is important to me. Afterwards, it's important to meet with them to show that you can leave the issue behind and not let it damage our relationship.

We can look at the qualities of a graduate in relation to each characteristic. For me, the crucial question is: does it all add up to the graduate being a person of faith? That is not to say that someone cannot be a very fine person without faith, but that the marker for a complete appropriation of the characteristics is growth in their personal relationship with God.

Michael Sheil SJ is Rector of Clongowes Wood College SJ and spiritual father to Third Line, First and Second year.

INDIVIDUAL CARE: EACH STUDENT MATTERS!

'DO I MATTER?'

A fundamental human question is: 'Do I matter?' The late writer and journalist Nuala O'Faolain in her autobiography *Are You Somebody?* describes being at a supermarket check-out when another customer looked across at her and asked innocently, 'Are you somebody?'[38]

For whom am I *somebody*? I matter to my family, friends and colleagues. On a broader level, whether recognised or not, I matter to the world: I am not simply a statistic, I have my unique role in the drama of life. Most radically, I matter to God – I am a daughter or son of God, God's beloved. But to experience the truth that I matter at every stage of life, I need the affirmation and care of others. Individual personal care, if we are fortunate, comes early to us from our parents. God, who is personal care itself, entrusts our development to other human beings, primarily our parents; if they fail, God tries to provide us with others who will ensure our growth.

Care and concern for the individual are therefore a hallmark of Jesuit education. The Latin term is *cura personalis*. It promotes the holistic growth of every student. Jesuit education thus suits every person, of whatever background. So far as resources allow, we provide a tailor-made education for each. We try to ensure that no pupil ever feels that she or he falls short of some abstract norm and so becomes of less importance. No individual, however problematic, is rejected for failing to 'measure up' to a standard established by the majority. While we commend progress and excellence, we are wary of competitiveness. In a sense, we can say that every student has 'special needs' and that we are all 'late developers'.

In *Far From the Tree* Andrew Solomon provides a nuanced study of the struggle of young people for identity. Gay, dyslexic and depressive himself, he discusses how our differences can be regarded either as disabilities to be treated or identities to be accepted. Not to be allowed one's identity can be disastrous, as in the case of an autistic child who believed that his parents did not want him – they wanted someone like him, but without his autism. This book has been called a Bill of Rights for those who differ from 'the norm'. In the context of this characteristic about the individual care due to each student, Solomon's work makes encouraging reading. It also reveals the demands made on parents and others – including teachers – to expand their hearts in order to embrace the, sometimes awkward, individuality of their child.[39]

Human individuality is a facet of God displayed in human form. Thomas Merton recounts an experience when standing on the corner of a busy shopping mall in Louisville, Kentucky: 'It was as if I suddenly saw the secret beauty of their hearts, the core of their reality, the person that each one is in God's eyes. If only they could all see themselves as they really are. If only we could see each other that way all the time!'[40]

CHALLENGE TO TEACHERS

Individual, personal care requires that teachers become as conversant as possible with the life experience of their students. Human experience is the starting point in Jesuit education. But, since this never occurs in a vacuum, teachers need to understand the world of the learner, including the influences of family, friends, peers and the larger society. It is within these parameters that learning will take place.

Teaching is a process of accompaniment – we use what helps this person; we adapt or put aside what may be obstructing the learning process. School structures are in service of the student: the school does not shape its students to fit itself, nor does it grind them out on a production line at year's end. Instead, systems, schedules, structures and methods are in service of relationships. While there are limits on how far individual needs can be met, the ideal remains to help each pupil to reach the fullness of her or his potential. Individual counselling and spiritual guidance are further expressions of this characteristic.

Care of the individual includes the encouraging and challenging of students to develop their unique competences, and to use their learning well – to understand, apply, analyse, synthesise and evaluate. They are motivated not to mouth the words and beliefs of others, but to find their own voices and trust in their own consciences. In this way they develop a lifelong ability to use their unique experiences as opportunities for growth.

The search for *meaning* is another way of searching for God – see the first characteristic discussed above. We cultivate the unique imagination of each pupil to recognise the real, the true, the beautiful, and to be open to wonder, awe and mystery, and to those 'Ah!' moments when they see in a new and transforming way. A rich imagination can make them open to believe that there is more to themselves than meets the eye, no matter what others think. It moves them beyond the platitudes of a tired and narrow culture. It opens out endless horizons and makes them into lifelong learners. Even death can be imagined as encompassed by a life that never ends, and this is grounded in the reality of Christ's resurrection. Here the search for meaning finally comes to fulfilment, and the profound importance of each individual is eternally validated.

IGNATIUS AND IMAGINATION

Imagination is unique to each human being, and is a facet of divine imagination. A well-developed imagination is open to the fullness of reality. This is what Aristotle, and the medieval Christian thinkers who followed him, were getting at by saying 'the soul is, in a way, all the things that exist'.[41] By this they meant that there is no aspect of reality excluded from the reach of imagination.

Imagination is a key player in the Ignatian view of what an individual can become. Ignatius himself had a vivid imagination, and could enter fully into the details of the life of Jesus, an experience that won him over totally to the love and service of Jesus and his Church. He was aware that he had been dealt with delicately and personally by God – 'as a schoolmaster deals with a child, teaching him', as he put it.[42] God kept placing images before, him until he caught on and reached the intended insights. Our methods of teaching must proceed along the same path. Care for an individual must mean connecting with that person's imagination, and encouraging their next feasible step forward.

As leader of the newly born Society of Jesus, Ignatius had a unique capacity to identify people of imagination. He would cultivate them individually until they were ready to encounter in a transforming way the Jesus of the New Testament. Imagination plays a key part in his retreat manual, the Spiritual Exercises. He tells us: *Imagine! Imagine the scenes of Jesus' life, death and resurrection. Enter into them as a participant, not a mere spectator.* Many of those he guided in this path were won over not only in mind and will but also in sensibility, desire, emotion and affectivity. They were then ready to be sent anywhere in the world in God's service. They had truly become *companions of Jesus*, the original term for the Jesuit Order.

Ignatius' preference throughout his life for one-to-one encounters helps to explain the emphasis in Jesuit education on personal care. Ignatius spent countless hours with individuals in spiritual conversation and in the giving of the Exercises. He said in 1536 that he could find no other work so fruitful and grace-filled than this. When visiting his home town for the last time, in 1535, he said he hoped to 'help people' through catechising them. His brother warned him that he would get nowhere, and Ignatius gently responded, 'If I could help only one, it would be enough'.[43] This is *cura personalis* in its essence. It mirrors the Gospel story about focusing on the sheep that is lost (Luke 15:3–6).

IMAGINATION AND FAITH

Blessed Cardinal Newman claimed long ago that 'the heart is commonly reached, not through the reason, but through the imagination'.[44] Michael Paul Gallagher proposes that the importance of imagination in stirring and nourishing a life of faith has too long been ignored.[45] He suggests that imagination may well be the new battleground of faith. We must recover the power of imagination and of receptive wonder. These, when well cultivated, can lead us forward into Mystery. Then we can find our way through the false images that compete for our hearts and minds, and nourish ourselves on what is truly worthwhile. Seamus Heaney's poem 'The Rain Stick' shows how imagination can take us beyond the threshold of the ordinary into new possibilities. It begins: 'Upend the rain stick and what happens next/Is a music that you never would have known/To listen for ...'[46]

THE THEOLOGY OF UNIQUENESS

The Gospels, perhaps especially St John's, are rich in one-to-one encounters between Jesus and individuals – examples of divine individual care for struggling humans. Through contemplating such events and reflecting on his own experience, Ignatius became convinced that God encounters each of us directly, and he demands that givers of the Exercises allow God and the individual to negotiate directly with one another, without interference. He recognised that each person is uniquely made in the image of God.

Each person is important to God, God's work of art and masterpiece. God therefore relates to each of us with individual care. Within this perspective, each of us has a unique role to play in the world's development, and God works to shape for each the opportunities to fulfil his or her singular role. We shall see below, in dealing with the characteristics of *community*, that our individual uniqueness lies within our membership of the body of humankind, which is also the Body of Christ. God's providential care for the world is total and comprehensive, and within that there operates God's care for each of us. Individual and corporate are dynamically interwoven.

A final note: while pupils *receive* individual care, they are also challenged to show it to the other members of the school community.

SUMMARY

Students develop best when they are in a learning environment that enables them to experience their own value to teachers, peers and the larger society. Hence Jesuit education emphasises individual care and concern for all.

Each student is unique and has a particular gift to bring to the human community.

The student's environment, background and potential for development are important areas for the teacher's reflection.

Through the environment and activities of our schools, we help students to grow holistically – to think for themselves, develop their diverse competences, find their own voices and claim their own identities.

Imagination opens the door to mystery, and inside we find that reality is imbued with the hidden presence of God.

INDIVIDUAL CARE: EACH STUDENT MATTERS!

LIVING EXPERIENCE

LIVING EXPERIENCE

SEEING THE BEST IN STUDENTS
Clare Broderick

The Jesuit characteristic of *cura personalis*, which translates as care of the whole person, suggests individualised attention to the needs of students, and an appropriate appreciation for singular gifts and uniqueness. *Cura personalis* is a phrase I have heard used on a regular basis since I joined Belvedere College. I believe it is an extremely important characteristic of Jesuit education: the individual care, attention and, dare I say, love that we hope each student experiences during his time in the college allows him to grow, make mistakes and develop into a 'man for others' as he graduates from Belvedere.

As a teacher of religious education I have seen *cura personalis* being shown to students on various retreats, social justice activities and pilgrimages in the college. But in terms of daily life in a busy, bustling secondary school my greatest understanding of it is in the role of form tutor. Each class group in Belvedere is assigned a form tutor for the entirety of their time in the college. In my eyes, the role of form tutor is the strongest example of this characteristic in action. Seeing 28 individuals on their first day in Belvedere and knowing that you will watch these individuals leave the college as men in six years' time is quite an experience, but it instils in me a responsibility to recognise the individuality of each of the students in my form group. Essentially the form tutor is a guide and mentor for each student in his care.

The challenge for me is to remind myself on a daily basis that I have a duty of care, as each child is created 'in the image of God' (Genesis 1:27). It is about encouraging, nurturing, supporting the student and recognising his individual strengths and gifts. I like to think of it as meeting each student where he is, not where I perceive he *should* be. Before writing this piece I asked a number of students, ranging from second to fifth year, about the purpose of having a form tutor. The responses were all of a similar nature: 'He looks after us' ... 'Our tutor looks out for us and cares about us' … 'We are listened to and know we have someone to support us' … 'She sees the best in us'.

Part of the role of form tutor entails challenging students, encouraging them to embrace all their gifts and talents, to step out of their comfort zone and engage in different experiences in order to enrich their lives and live them to the full. The tutor enables each student to recognise that to be himself is more than enough, that he can value his uniqueness and realise his power to share his talents with others. In the words of Marianne Williamson, 'We are all meant to shine, as children do. We were born to make manifest the glory of God that is within us. It's not just in some of us; it's in everyone.'[47]

Living out *cura personalis*, be it as a religious education teacher or form tutor can be an extremely rewarding experience. The relationship that develops over the six years between the tutor and student can be quite special. However, it is not without challenges; I am human and have made mistakes. Encouraging some students to 'go forth and set the world on fire' may not be the easiest of tasks. The biggest challenge for me today is time. As the teaching day is so very full, finding the opportunity to check in with students and encourage them on a regular basis is becoming more difficult.

Clare Broderick is a teacher of religious education and form tutor at Belvedere College SJ.

HOME ECONOMICS AND *CURA PERSONALIS*
Jen Condon

Over the years, I have been asked by many of my students what my job is like – usually by those students interested in a career teaching home economics themselves. I always reply that I have the best job in the world. This usually causes confusion: am I being serious? After all, how many people say that about their jobs? I mean real, normal jobs, not the variety they come up with when asked their dream careers: mattress tester, chocolate taster, and so on. I never thought during my teacher training that being a teacher of home economics could be such a rewarding and fulfilling experience. When I reflect on why this is, it all comes down to Jesuit education and Ignatian spirituality.

To me, the most important characteristic of Jesuit Education is *cura personalis*. This underlies all the other characteristics and is palpable in everything we do. It means care and concern for each and every individual who comes through our doors. We help them to grow morally, personally and spiritually. We try to help each student develop holistically, to find their own voice, to accept and celebrate their unique identities. This is particularly difficult for teenagers who are painfully aware of standing out and do not want to be unique at all!

There is an emphasis in our school on social outreach and charitable work. One of the programmes running successfully for many years is called 'Fast Friends'. In their home economics module, Transition Year students meet students from another school once a week for a double class. These students are the same age as Crescent students, but suffer from various health issues. Many have speech and language difficulties, which challenge good communication. Others have Down's Syndrome or autism, or may be confined to wheelchairs. During the module, Crescent students work with their fast friends to prepare a dish in the kitchen, eat it together and clean up together. Because of time constraints, there is always pressure to concentrate, stay on task and get everything cleaned up on time. The emphasis is not just on developing skills, but on cooperating, acting as a team, and working within the boundaries of what their partner is capable of. Our students are taken out of their comfort zone, which is a challenge in itself. I check in with my students regularly to see how they are progressing and how the experience is measuring up to their expectations.

Last year, the group had done other subjects before taking their turn at home economics. They were getting along well, and I had been impressed by the way they gelled, as well as by the insights our students had gained. One day, I asked one of my students how he was getting on with his fast friend, and how he found the cookery module. I was informed that my student and his new friend – a particularly garrulous and bubbly young man – had been getting on well, but since the beginning of the cookery module my student had noticed that his friend was 'very stubborn'. He could not understand or appreciate my delight until I explained: my student was no longer seeing his fast friend as a 'special' person, someone he had to talk to slowly and always allow to win at games. He was finally seeing his fast friend as a real person, a person with flaws, imperfections and personality traits that had nothing to do with his condition. Thereafter, the module became more meaningful because the relationship had become more real.

I have seen this happen time and again within 'Fast Friends'. Students are challenged to step out of their comfort zone and to grow. Just the other day, I checked in with a student. He had had doubts about the module initially, and had taken a few weeks to really get involved. He told me that he was enjoying it far more than he anticipated. He had never thought that he would be good with those with special needs. Another student is now considering a career in special needs teaching. None of these students had any previous experience in this area, but have come away with newfound respect for its challenges.

Teaching home economics at Crescent really is the best job in the world! Here we help our students to discover their talents and to develop holistically. We promote the development of the personal, emotional and spiritual self: definitely more rewarding than a career as a mattress tester!

Jen Condon is a home economics teacher at Crescent College Comprehensive SJ.

SHOWING STUDENTS YOU CARE
A conversation with Éamonn Davis SJ

You can show students you care by talking with them: it's all about relationships. When you talk with them, one to one, they should leave you feeling ten foot tall.

If classes get a reputation for being difficult, I challenge them to 'prove them wrong'. I try to speak to the best in each of them, but one has to be firm. I let the lads know that they have to earn the things they want to do.

Even from a young age, I challenge them to show leadership. I give them guidelines. I tell them how to act like a teacher in the life-saving class. I make it clear that they do it my way when they are in the swimming-pool as instructors. I want them to praise those they are teaching, for effort as well as results. They are to respect everyone, knowing their names and attending to everyone in the class. They must be well prepared, and I have a checklist to help them and a hand-out with the list of things that need to be ready for the class.

It's not enough that a student should be very good himself; I ask them to give something back. If they are capable of getting a distinction then they are expected to give something back to others. They must be inclusive. From a very young age, they are ready to take on leadership. I challenge them by saying, 'You are the instructor, what do *you* think?'

I have taken many groups to Lourdes. Along with the hard work, the long hours, the sleepless nights and the friendship, some of them experience great peace at the grotto. Each evening we share our experiences and reflect on the day. It's the same with the Kairos retreats; it brings them closer to the person of Jesus.

Even the experience of running some of the activities can give them great experience and foster belief in themselves. I remember one summer a young lad came to me looking for funds for the soup run over the summer. I gave him €400. He walked out of the office amazed, telling others 'he trusted me with that money'. He couldn't get over it; it did him the world of good.

The picture in in my office of the laughing Jesus is very popular. One boy said that in a period when his family had trouble he reminded them of that picture and it kept them going. Another boy wrote to me after 6th Year. He said that he used to sit at the back of the class during Vincent de Paul meetings and duck down and hide whenever I looked for a volunteer. He was so shy he seldom talked to anyone. One day as he slipped out I nabbed him and said, 'Mrs So and So needs a visit and you're just the man'. He went over to her and the visit changed his whole life. Now he is going to University and feels great. The lady rang me on the morning of his Graduation here and asked could she come as he was the nicest boy she had every met in her life.

Sometimes you get an idea and follow a hunch. You never know what effect it will have.

Éamonn Davis SJ is a chaplain at Belvedere College SJ.

CURA PERSONALIS
A conversation with Juliette Frost

I work 'one to one' with first to third year students. Crescent was the first school where I taught, and I was immediately struck by the atmosphere and the easy relationships between teachers and students. It's very professional, but friendly; they seem to know each other really well from school activities. It's a very different atmosphere from what I experienced myself as a pupil. New parents or teachers would be reassured if they knew this.

There is a strong culture of 'looking out' for other people. That's a real value here. Amongst the students there is a great rapport and you can see that they take notice of one another. For example, if a student is unwell he or she waits in the main area to be taken home by a parent. You will see teachers and students checking with the pupil to see if he or she is all right.

Some students come to the school challenged by a particular disability. You can see how the school community, although initially a bit unsure as to how to react, tries to reach out, so that they are included. The students find their own little ways of communicating, whether it's a 'thumbs up' sign, or a pat on the arm as they pass, or maybe assisting them getting around. Most importantly, the students can flourish and feel part of the community and the parents are delighted that their child is happy.

There are great opportunities here for all the students. They become well rounded, and well able to get on with things. They are not perfect, it's not the perfect school – there are the ups and downs, but I am talking about the general atmosphere.

I think the support that pupils get to fulfil themselves gives them great confidence. They have the chance to develop their various talents and there are options beyond the academic. I see it in the senior pupils. They are mature and well able to engage in conversation by the time they are in sixth year. They come across as sorted out and confident in themselves, with deep friendships that remain beyond their school years. Those skills are a great help for life. The fact that the school is co-educational gives them confidence in a mixed environment and enables friendships to grow. They are mature enough to pop back into the school to visit after they leave and get a great kick if they are invited into the staff room.

Great support is shown to new staff. In the staffroom everyone makes an effort to make you welcome; it's very daunting at first, so we all try to make it easier. I know I appreciated that when I started. Everyone gets on with things but there is great support and there is a sense of a shared goal, which is *to be there for* the students. Senior teachers are supportive of new ones. There is a great willingness also to hear the parents' points of view. Everyone tries to give of their best – and when you do that, you also know that you are just 'doing your job'.

Juliette Frost is a special needs assistant at Crescent College Comprehensive SJ.

THE WATER DISPENSER
Ann Guinee

Each person is known and loved personally by God and so we begin a search for the destiny and meaning of our lives in freedom and in the company of the other believers. So Jesuit education emphasises the uniqueness of each person and encourages a lifelong openness to keep growing … in search of the will of Him who loves unconditionally.[48]

It may seem a little odd that my starting point for talking about my work with students here and the characteristics of Jesuit education is the water dispenser that sits in the corner behind the door of my office. But then, when I consider how often water features in the Gospels and in Old Testament stories, the connection can be appreciated.

My office used to belong to Administration. In the good old days before embargoes curtailed us, sick, tired or upset students were cared for here. Caring sometimes took the form of a little first aid or a phone call home, but more frequently it meant five minutes out of class to sit and sip a cup of cool water. In recent years the room was most often shut as money to pay teachers for these extra hours was cut: first aid is at present kindly administered by the office staff. When I first asked to have this room in the heart of the school as the Student Support office it was suggested that I get rid of the water dispenser, but I found myself determined to keep it. This watering hole, reappearing in the middle of the central area was something of an oasis in the desert, with students gathering frequently to drink their fill. The Student Support role, as well as the office, was open for business.

It's not easy to ask for support. My role is to support students who are identified as disadvantaged in a variety of ways; academically, socially, culturally, economically. Any of these factors can increase the risk that a student may disengage from education and leave school early. I have a core group who are already part of a school completion programme when they come to the Crescent. However, for these and others to ask for specific support is to accept a label that was never part of their identity as they feel and live it.

But, to come for a drink of water is the most natural thing in the world. And, boy, are they thirsty! So they come and fill up their cups and bottles and as they do so they fall into conversation. They tell me about their day, their classes, their teachers, their weekends, their families, their relationships; and somewhere along the way needs are identified and aids are supplied or interventions organised. Yet something much more profound is occurring in these interactions. The students are letting themselves be seen. Their personalities come through as they share about their lives, their homes and families, their interests and hobbies, their talents, their animals, their difficulties and frustrations, their expectations, their sense of justice and injustice, their self-consciousness and their pride. And these bigger pictures that they offer transcend expectations and labels.

They reveal what is unique, unpredictable, deeply fascinating and significant about each and every one of them.

As I sit in discovery, I am awed by talents as yet unknown to the school – riding, horse training, boxing, mechanics, buying and selling. I am constantly reminded that I know nothing, really, in the light of their knowledge of dogs and horses, how to make health drinks from seaweed collected on the beach, hunting, fishing, how to accept tragedy and hardship, how 'family' has many working variations, how to diagnose and fix problems with my car, also how best to make it rev, the proper terms for speaking about pop and rap music, drug awareness, how to take care of young children or sick uncles. And in a world where they are often asked and expected somehow to overcome who they are in order to fit in with systems which put them in a marginalised group, my job is to take all their shining and bend school life a little to reflect it, in line with the Jesuit characteristic of celebrating the uniqueness of every person.

In return, I get an office decorated by rosettes and medals from equestrian competitions in which these students have proudly and ably represented their school. I get the satisfaction of hearing them speak at assembly and seeing them feature regularly in the school newsletter alongside the rugby, hockey and science heroes. I enjoy a homework skills group, which often opts to stay on long after homework is done to play board-games and chat. I have readers who vet, in their own terms, the novels I buy for students and teach me about those terms for my next purchases. At a minimum, I have learnt, novels have to grab the attention on the first page and use everyday language. I have opportunities to build links with communities, which are accepting of our school's need to learn and desire to help. And, maybe best of all, I have a car whose doors no longer squeak and stick, thanks to a thorough oiling administered by two students who provide a steady supply of wise tips about car maintenance and driving. I am awed by what I might have thought was ordinary; I am opened to the presence of God in all things and led by example into a proper understanding of holistic education.

Water, meeting place, insight, teaching and learning ... you can't help think of Christ after all. Long live the water dispenser!

Ann Guinee is a Student Support Worker at Crescent College Comprehensive SJ.

THE ETHOS OF INCLUSIVENESS
Val Hamilton

Care for the individual is key to what we are involved with in the Special Education Needs (SEN) department. Students who fall within certain criteria, laid out by the National Council for Special Education (NCSE), are allocated additional teaching support hours per week, according to their individualised needs. These hours are provided as an integral part of their education in school. Some students, who do not meet the criteria laid down by the NCSE, also receive support from the SEN team and mainstream staff, under Learning Support guidelines.

There are many avenues to realising the potential of students in addition to the actual hours allocated to subject assistance. I have a number of students diagnosed with emotional and social difficulties, and I work with them to discuss these needs and I also provide support in particular subject areas. For students on the Autistic Spectrum, we provide assistance in their interaction with peers and their communication skills. We help our students to view their potential in a very positive way: our interaction style is to be very proactive, even dealing with grades – 'That is what you got, where can we go with this?'

Because we are a Jesuit school and are inspired by the Ignatian ethos – and especially by the characteristic of care for the person, I find that we are given an additional opportunity to expand our role. The care for the individual is the base, so there is more possibility and added flexibility in our approach, than perhaps in other post-primary settings. There is a keen desire to see how we can perform better, to support a student's individualised needs. I feel that this is due to our ethos. For example, how we use the available hours to support each student depends upon the targets that we agree upon

63

in collaboration with the student themselves, their parents and their form tutor.

Obviously I deal with numerous anxious parents. The strong academic reputation of Jesuit schools can cause anxiety to some. Parents may wonder if a student with special educational needs will fit in. Will he be able to cope with the curriculum and meet the academic standard, and how will he cope overall? We need to work around this; we need to be clear on what is available in terms of support. Our first role is to offer parents the assurance that their child will be supported to reach his potential, and what is done in the classroom will also be further supported by us, if necessary. We try to reassure parents that we, along with the rest of the staff will make every effort to support him through his six years, so that he will be able to make the most of his school experience.

Students can be wary too. They can be worried that their peers will learn about their needs. It takes them a while to adjust, especially the first years. In secondary school they want to guard their privacy, and their priority is to fit in with peers, not to stand out. Their view of support is formed by their experience, or lack of it, in primary level. Some would mainly have experienced computer programmes, designed for learning support, with aptitude testing on a regular basis, to check if they have improved. We want to support our students through the *full* curriculum.

Acceptance throughout the school of the Jesuit ethos of inclusiveness, of acceptance, of variety, of difference and diversity, makes our work easier. In my time here I have seen us grow from a tentative start, because the school was seen as primarily academic. In the beginning, people had reservations about SEN. The Jesuit ethos has helped us grow to a deeper understanding of how to be inclusive. Respecting difference is a very big part of how we approach things in the school. We started on this path, not knowing exactly how it would work. I think you can say that no one knew, and for us there was growth and discovery, guided by the characteristic of care for the person, and an inner sense for what felt 'right'. It is now ten years since the department was founded on a permanent basis.

In a practical way, we are in a very positive frame of mind at present – the group of students with SEN, who left the school this year, did very well: some had considerable learning needs and it was hard to predict how they would do in their Leaving Cert. They joined the school when the department was up and running for four years. They stayed with the school and we feel that they not only realised their potential, but many exceeded their own expectations. It was a wonderful moment to realise that building trust with each individual, helping them to grow in all aspects as persons, had helped them to open that doorway to a future that each student had identified for himself. Some had a wish list and achieved the items on it. Others got their first choice. So that was a great moment for us and for many of their teachers. As part of the whole school staff, our SEN department played an important role in supporting the individuals under our care, who left the school smiling. Box ticked!

Val Hamilton is a special educational needs co-coordinator at Belvedere College SJ.

THE HEART OF CHILD-CENTRED EDUCATION
A conversation with Jo Anne Hanrahan

When I was asked about this book, and whether I would contribute, I said 'you have the wrong person!' Then I was told, 'Just talk about what you are doing!'

I took a career break from the Crescent some time ago. That was when I really realised how much the school meant to me: I missed it so much, the contact with the students and how we do things. The rapport between students and teachers is very special; it's great. I suppose you could say many schools aim for this. I had taught before; this was not my first school. But I very quickly found that my personal values and the values of the school coincided – I could say to myself 'I am in the right place here'. I always felt that child-centred education was very important. I see this as self-evident, but it is not always treated as a key objective in other places. Here the student is really valued.

At the start of the year you have to be so conscious of the new children. You watch out for little things, smoothing over difficulties, making sure they don't feel too lost in the new set up. Coming here is a massive change for them. They begin to recognise you in the corridors. You hope that maybe by showing kindness to them that it will rub off on them. They begin to understand that is how we do things here, and they also see that it's coming from our belief in them.

Other values resonate with me, especially the desire to develop the whole person. There is a great variety of activities and programmes. Every school wants to develop the whole student, but I find the teachers here give each other, and the students, greater support in trying to achieve that.

One of the Social Outreach programmes with which I am involved is the 'Fast Friends' programme. There is great interest in this programme and strong support for it throughout the school. It has been in operation now for 25 years. It was set up by a PE teacher from this school and a teacher from a Special Needs school in town. Basically, it centres on a weekly visit for an hour with someone who has special needs. A two-way relationship is established. Some keep in touch over time; others make a career choice based on this experience.

If you take students out of their comfort zone, they learn things very quickly. Some may have had a wide variety of experiences, especially if they travel abroad with their families. But the outreach programme always takes them outside their comfort zone. They might have skiied before, but it's being asked to be a leader or to take charge of first aid that gives a different emphasis and makes it a fresh experience for them. We take a group camping to Achill: they have to negotiate with others, say taking turns to charge phones, and so forth. They get wise quickly when they are challenged with experiences they have never had before, maybe more rough-and-tumble than they are used to. Then they begin to wonder what the experience is all about. The basis that was laid in the earlier years in the school serves them well: they have the skills to cope. Afterwards they take great pride in what they have done.

I love the opportunity that PE, especially gymnastics, gives: it allows different skills to emerge. The students get experience of working in little groups. They discover there are different ways to do things and that this is all right. Whether working in unison or one by one, they see that. Everyone is made to feel that their contribution is worthwhile, and they see that. They become comfortable with each other. This extends to accepting people of different abilities or with special needs. They are all part of the community and it is wonderful to see how welcoming the students are, and willing to make a special effort for others. They learn that everyone has the right to come in happy and to leave happy. Sometimes you are aware that they are unhappy when they come in, but you always hope that they leave happy.

As part of the Jesuit tradition we ask them to reflect frequently on what they are doing. This is a key issue: life is not just a matter of dashing through new experiences; it's a chance to absorb the experience and examine how it affects them. We teachers find we learn so much from their reflections. In adjusting programmes I go back over these reflections and find great depth in them. They help to shape the future.

The nine characteristics are all threaded through the work we do, but for me the overriding one is individual care, it is at the heart of child-centred education. It is the core value and the rest are all related to it. I find that it gets into all my thinking; I am living it, even when I'm away. It has become part of me.

Jo Anne Hanrahan is a teacher of PE, geography and social outreach at Crescent College Comprehensive SJ.

GROWING IN RESPONSIBLE FREEDOM

HAPPINESS

*'Tell me, what is it you plan to do
With your one wild and precious life?'*[49]

Mary Oliver's challenging lines offer an entry point into the third characteristic of Jesuit education. God loves and respects the growing freedom of each child. No system or individual has the right to subvert this – it is God's precious gift. God will always respect human freedom, so we want our pupils to grow into mature free individuals. Since all human abilities and attributes are ambiguous – they can be used for good or bad – we speak here of *responsible* freedom. We want students to develop the capacity to shape their lives in line with the highest human values.

The European Social Survey (ESS) is a social-scientific project that maps the attitudes, beliefs and behaviour patterns of the various populations in Europe.[50] Over several decades it has shown that freedom itself is the highest value for many people. But is the human person autonomous, free to decide everything to his or her own advantage? Christian faith offers a broader vision than that. Ignatius proposes that as created beings we belong to Another. This Other gives us the gift of freedom so that we may reach the fullness of human happiness, which is the enjoyment of divine life within a transfigured humanity. Our task, Ignatius says, is to make our decisions in the light of what God desires for us. Freedom is at its best when it serves both the common and the individual good. While the urge for autonomy insists that the self be placed at the centre of our world, the Christian view is that we live rightly only by interdependence, and in a world of which God is the centre. This is a theocentric as against an anthropological world-view.

We have noted that happiness was a primary goal for Aristotle. It remains such in the Christian vision. But instead of being at the mercy of subjective whim and judgement, happiness now has a definite specification. It consists in being in harmony with God, who is Happiness Itself. Not that a divine blueprint for happiness exists somewhere, which we ignore at our peril, but that God has a staggeringly vast project for human happiness and wants us to collaborate creatively and freely to achieve it. We would rightly fear a god who would take away our freedom, but the real God, having given us the gift of freedom, wants us only to enhance it.

WHAT GOD INTENDS

The divine project is profound and demanding. What God intends here and now is the development of the community of humankind. God intends a new world order, embracing and going beyond the best of human desire. This new community is to be universally characterised by good and just relationships; everyone is to be respected and included; the world's resources are for equitable sharing. Jesus worked, was killed and rose again to create this community. He called it the 'Kingdom of God' – this term sounds distant today, so let us find alternatives if needed, such as 'a civilisation of mutual love' or 'a universal culture of love'. We need to forge terms that reveal the richness and complexity of a dynamic situation in which divine love is all in all. Since religious language always falls short of the reality it intends to convey, an endless process of translation is required to communicate well what God has in mind.

In this divinely orchestrated environment, however we name it, each is watching out for the others in mutual concern. Everyone is included and cherished. Forgiveness and amendment operate to overcome division and greed. All members are enabled to grow to the fullness of their potential and generously to put their talents at the service of others. In this mutual service we all become fully ourselves. The common good takes priority over personal happiness and also leads to it. We take joy in the joy of others, for happiness is essentially enjoyed in common.

This gives an idea of what 'responsible freedom' can mean. The goal of Ignatius' *Spiritual Exercises* is to help people towards freedom, so that their decisions are not contaminated by what he calls 'inordinate attachments' (*Spiritual Exercises*, n.1). The love that moves us in our decision-making must come not from self-centred motivation but from God. It is thus that we move even now beyond our blinkered horizons into the divine dimension of reality. The desire of God is that people be happy not only after death but in this present world. This underlies the urgency in Jesus' call to us to conduct all interactions within the horizon of the divine. 'May Your kingdom come – now!'

WHAT WORLD?

The world into which young people are growing is an arena of competing values. Within it our educational enterprise operates, drawing on the vision and hope that Christian faith provides.

The chaos underlying human life in so many aspects is endlessly exposed in the daily news. There is a massive struggle around authentic living. Relationships between God and humankind are radically distorted. We are alienated from ourselves, from our neighbour, from the environment and from God. The wound that used to be called original sin runs deep. The Christian response is that these fractured relationships have already been radically healed in Christ. In friendship with him we are empowered to love God, to love ourselves rightly and to love others, including 'enemies'. We are to exercise sensitive stewardship of the planet entrusted to us, and to play our part in 'the universal restoration' (Acts 3:21).

Cold reason judges people by how they fit into economic and social categories. In some schemes, the human person is merely 'economic man' (*homo economicus*). Thus many are classed as unfit for purpose and millions of the poor are unwanted because they are surplus to requirements. Such greed, exclusion and heartlessness are countered by Christian compassion and the Golden Rule, 'Do to others as you would wish them to do to you'. Economics can be relational, through justice, sharing and cooperation. Corporate greed is challenged by Catholic social teaching, which is profoundly critical of current market-driven economies and the injustices that they perpetuate.[51]

The narrowing of horizons to intra-worldly perspectives means that absolute values lose their foundation. This leads individuals to carve out for themselves what they can. Against this view, Christian faith steadily proclaims that humankind is already orientated towards God's final community of love. There we will find the fulfilment of our deepest desires. Against rampant exploitation of our natural resources, we are challenged to care for the environment and to restore right relationships with creation, which is our present and future home. We form one community of humankind, and so true education must develop a global perspective.

The Christian vision constitutes the historical response of God to our inhumanity towards one another. In the face of our endemic inability for sustained development, God is already calling us to participate in the divine project of care for humankind, for the individual and for the environment. God has initiated this project in Jesus Christ, the Man for Others, who is described simply as the One who 'went about doing good' (Acts 10:38). This is our task too. The Churches are challenged to be in embryo that civilisation of loving care of which God dreams.

Long ago Plato said, 'Life is a risk, but a beautiful risk!'[52] Christian living is a greater risk, but even more beautiful, in its challenge and its reward. The Christian vision for humankind will not be achieved within the bounds of human history. But a trans-worldly destiny beckons us. We are invited to play our part in its achievement; confident that in ways unknown to us God will make all things well.

GROWTH

Our schools orientate pupils toward responsible freedom, which is to be realised in participative action for the good of others as well as care for oneself. This involves a process of steady and patient growth. Growth infers that the student is not expected to have fully arrived, but is in process. There can be no forced growth, especially in religious matters. Growth is for the long haul, and we cannot set its limits. It includes the capacity for adapting to expanding horizons through the progressive exercising of freedom and responsibility. In dealing with individual care we discussed the task of fostering well-cultivated imaginations so as to help students reach out to the infinite. Without imagination, little sustained growth is possible. Growth is not limited to the intellectual, affective, moral and physical dimensions, but includes that of the spirit. A spirituality of openness to the Beyond is needed. Around the time that CS Lewis was proposing that a new step in evolution had taken place with the Incarnation,[53] Teilhard de Chardin was writing *The Phenomenon of Man*, a sweeping outline of the slow growth of humankind to its fullness in Christ.[54]

By exploring with them their own images and languages, we can help students to articulate their dynamic urge to become more themselves. They know something of love, self-respect, friendship, gratitude, tenderness, acceptance, truth, forgiveness. They experience happiness and sorrow, friendship and love, the ups and downs of relationships, sexuality and loneliness. Death and bereavement can come close to them, and they are acquainted with suffering, whether their own or in wider society. 'The thoughts of youth are long, long thoughts ...' and we can encourage our students to reflect on the richness and the mystery of their unfolding experience.[55]

FRIENDSHIP AND LOVE

The capacity for love is a key area of growth. We work for the enlargement not only of the mind but also of the heart. We are intrinsically relational beings, and friendship opens us up to this world of relationships and hints at the Beyond. With true friendship comes the reverent amazement that expresses itself in the simple phrase, *I am loved!* This gives rise to the profound question - *why should this love be given me?* To be loved is always a surprise, liberating and challenging. The experience of being loved awakens our depths, and we become participants in the drama of living, rather than spectators. Already related to the universe in its magnificence simply by being in existence, we now enter into the domain of personal relationships. Growth in authentic human love raises the question: *is there yet more than this?* And an affirmative response brings us into the world of God, who *is* love itself. Thus we come to relate to God by exploring our basic human experiences of loving.

GROWING IN FAITH

The pure desire to know is innate. We are beings who seek meaning throughout the dimensions of our humanity. The term 'Ignatian humanism' indicates an attitude of unrestricted openness to the created world: it affirms that we live in a universe of grace, and that God is immersed in all creation and human endeavour. In this view, the human and the religious are not mutually exclusive worlds, but interwoven. Religious language at its most meaningful springs from the fundamental themes of human experience. The step to the transcendent is not a giant one: it is possible to explore the divine.

Belief is native to us, as is trust. Today, human commitment and, even more, religious commitment can seem unwise and restrictive, but if we see the Gospel message as a radical call to the fullness of reality, things change. Faith is the God-given way of rightly understanding existence. The disorder we bring about in human affairs is re-ordered by the gospel. While there is no merely human solution to the human predicament of decline, there is a divine remedy and it is already operative.[56] God's task is to make humankind truly human, and Jesus Christ, in the Christian view, is the exemplar of what the human person can become. God provides a new and intelligible horizon for the wrong-doing, violence, sin, suffering and death that scar our world. God's world is spacious and accommodates the full scope of human reality. Hence the importance of this third characteristic: it saves us from placing limits to human growth, because mystery beckons us, and our fulfilment is in the divine.

SUMMARY

The gift of freedom empowers us to shape constructively and responsibly our own lives and those of others.

The happiness God intends for us is unlimited. We grow towards this happiness by becoming attuned to God's presence in our lives.

The divine dream for humankind is a new world order in which everyone is enabled to participate fully and grow to the fullness of their potential.

Our students learn to reflect on the rich mystery hidden in their personal experiences of life, especially those of love. This is their path to the Beyond.

The Christian vision offers a persuasive response to the human predicament of decline. Students are challenged to grow in hope, and to bring Christian values to bear on the problems they encounter.

GROWTH IN RESPONSIBLE FREEDOM

LIVING EXPERIENCE

LIVING EXPERIENCE

TO BE DRAWN BEYOND THEMSELVES
Una Allen

I have four children, three sons and one daughter, all of whom attended **Coláiste Iognáid** Galway (The Jes) between the years 2000 and 2012. They are four very different individuals, yet they all have one thing in common – they all loved the Jes. Each would say, without reservation, that they would hope to send their own children there. They maintain that the school fostered a sense of dignity and respect between students and teachers, and also amongst the students themselves. It gave them a sense of confidence and freedom, and an ability to recognise and celebrate difference. It gave them a certain fearlessness in seeking justice for the underdog. As they reflect back on their years there, the resulting bond and consequent sense of loyalty and understanding continues to have a very strong connection for them.

For my own part I vividly remember, as a first time parent, being welcomed by the headmaster, and being told that in the Jes, the ethos of the school was that each child was unique, individual and loved by God. This sentiment proved to be the foundation stone of my experience of the school. It has stayed with me throughout my own children's education and beyond. It has permeated my own sense of parenting, and indeed my life. This idea of a personal God who loves us unconditionally, who wants to be involved in our lives and in the lives of our children, who is continually inviting and seeking a response, endlessly drawing us beyond ourselves if we are prepared to take the risk – I remember thinking, *this* is what I want for my children!

The impact of an educational system with such an ethos has helped them to achieve growth into responsible freedom. There is no doubt that the instilling of mutual respect and the fostering of the uniqueness of the person has been at the core of how they have begun to proceed through life. It has allowed them to form much deeper friendships at a young age than they might otherwise have done, and has shaped the way they think and how they treat others in day-to-day life.

Each of the children would say that, in the senior cycle especially, this mutual respect and trust came to the fore. They agree that it was unusual to find quiet in the classroom, and to the untutored eye it might appear that chaos sometimes reigned. The teachers allowed the students to talk amongst themselves, as long as the conversations pertained to the work in hand. The students would say that this promoted a culture of sharing knowledge, which was entirely collegiate. They were taught never to hoard their knowledge or their understanding of various topics but instead to share with their peers, so that they too could also understand. My own children would say that this particular aspect of school has been carried over into university and has allowed them to help peers who may have been struggling, not only in the academic sense but in other aspects of their lives. It has also enabled them to be unafraid to seek help themselves if needed.

There is no doubt that the teachers saw their students first as individual human beings, rather than as students or potential grades. This important distinction has taught the children to grasp the importance of the person, and to see the needs of the person as paramount.

I had personal experience of this when I worked as a probation officer in Galway. A number of years ago, prior to my own involvement in the school as a parent, there had been a spate of very nasty break-ins in the city. It emerged eventually that a gang of young people from various secondary schools – the Jes included – had been involved. The cases were put back for probation report and it was my task to compile the various reports for court. I remember going into the Jes early one Monday morning and being brought up through the school by the headmaster, through a teeming maelstrom of young people, all seemingly converging at the same time from everywhere. As we passed through the crowds, the headmaster greeted each one by his or her Christian name, and each student responded with a smile, stepping back to allow us to pass unimpeded. I was hugely impressed at the time; but what impressed me even more was that during those court cases – which entailed a number of appearances by the defendants over a period of months – from my recollection, alone, out of all the schools involved, the students from the Jes were *always* accompanied either by their headmaster or a senior teacher in a role of support. The teachers sat with their students in the body of the court. At the time I remember thinking that there must be something special about a school that was prepared to put its corporate head above the parapet and show support for its pupils, when everybody else seemed to be baying for blood over the nastiness of the crimes committed. Here it seemed everyone was to be respected, included and cherished, cared for out of a mutual concern. I now realise that what I was actually witnessing was a practical application of the characteristic of growing in responsible freedom.

Una Allen is a member of the Ignatian Identity Group and a former parent at Coláiste Iognáid SJ.

YOUR CHILDREN ARE NOT YOUR CHILDREN
Martin Beuster

Freedom is a challenging proposition. When the constraints and the security of authoritative guidance are falling away, the liberated world gets infinitely more complex and challenging. While it is not unique to parenting, this challenge is very much part of the parenting journey. For freedom is a gift that we offer each other, or not; it is reciprocal and always relational. It is very real as an experience. And it takes tremendous courage for parents to offer this freedom to their children. Khalil Gibran captured this poignantly in one of his poems:
Your children are not your children.
They are the sons and daughters of Life's longing for itself.
They come through you but not from you,
And though they are with you, yet they belong not to you.
You may give them your love but not your thoughts,
For they have their own thoughts.
You may house their bodies but not their souls,
For their souls dwell in the house of tomorrow, which you cannot visit,
not even in your dreams.

You may strive to be like them, but seek not to make them like you.
For life goes not backward nor tarries with yesterday.
You are the bows from which your children as living arrows are sent
*   forth.*
The archer sees the mark upon the path of the infinite, and He bends
*   you with His might that*
His arrows may go swift and far.
Let your bending in the archer's hand be for gladness;
For even as he loves the arrow that flies, so He loves also the bow that
*   is stable.*[57]

I remember how uncomfortable I felt when I first came across this poem. Here I was, with three young children: wild, wonderful, demanding, imaginative and full of life, stretching my resources to the limit, testing the boundaries. We were having great fun and living together out of an experience of shared pain and loss. And then I'm confronted with this line, 'Your children are not your children'. The sense of discomfort, which was intense, was mixed with a lingering curiosity growing from the resonance of words such as 'Life's longing for itself'. The idea that we may give them our love but not our thoughts seemed to make sense. But it took a lot of growing for me as a parent to claim the space and offer it to our children so that they might grow up as young people.

On his visit to Limerick a few years ago Fr Adolfo Nicolás SJ said that in his experience growth happens when things are not going to plan. Children in Rwanda inspired him to dance. Survivors of genocide, they were dancing.[58] We all have to face our moments of failure, rejection and loss; moments which can leave us bewildered, angry, sad, and sometimes despairing. But precisely in those moments we tend to encounter opportunities for getting to know ourselves better; sometimes we take them. What has helped me most was to see and to appreciate people who are just there, with a smile, or a cup of tea offered without any fuss, or a silent meeting of eyes for a moment longer than I had expected. Not much said, just a quiet accepting presence. Yes, things have gone wrong, but there will be another day. This is the space where questions are not asked, where pain is felt and acknowledged, and where forgiveness might be offered in an act of faith and trust in the other. When we can accept such forgiveness, offered without an expectation of anything in return, we will be prompted to respond to this experience with generosity.

Teenagers have a keen sensitivity to justice, and we would do well as adults to tune into their language, listen carefully and take them very seriously. I remember my son Daniel coming home from school one day when he was in fifth year, somewhat frustrated, annoyed and quite fidgety. He wasn't exactly rushing to the dinner table to sit with us; but when he did, a story began to emerge. A teacher whom he respected and worked well with had ridiculed one of his classmates with cynical remarks. And it had happened a few times. The kids in that class were annoyed, angry and frustrated, but did not know how to stop this. After some discussion at our table, Daniel decided to talk to the teacher, one-to-one, and tell him how he felt. It wasn't a comfortable chat; it was difficult for both of them. It took place between two people, at eye level, outside the dynamic of the classroom. Both of them had the courage to enter this space where they dared to speak and to listen to each other with honesty, and where they placed trust in each other. The chat helped to resolve the situation, and changed their relationship fundamentally.

Experiential learning is a slow burner; the alignment of experience and integration into our life happens at its own pace. It is not in our gift as parents to integrate the experience of our children. What we can do is listen to them carefully, share with them our efforts to reflect on our experience, and be present to their joy and pain when we are invited to do so. A lot of growing happens when we are not there, when the arrow has left the bow. This is both unsettling and reassuring. When we are free to let our children go, there will be privileged occasions when we witness how they grow and get a taste of the transformative power of truth.

Martin Beuster is a member of the Ignatian Identity Group and the parent of three former students at Coláiste Iognáid SJ.

LEARNING LIFE SKILLS
A conversation with Cian Browne

I have taught a wide variety of subjects as well as business. The value that really stands out for me is individual care, linked also to the values of 'being the best you can' and 'giving back'. Those three are huge for me. The idea of individual care creates a whole network of care here, it applies from pupil to pupil, obviously from teacher to pupil and also teacher to teacher – but likewise pupil to teacher.

I loved the school and I have found that there is a very strong bond between past pupils, a lasting relationship. I am still in touch with many of my own class, still best friends. We all agree that we had great fun while we were being educated, and that the teachers were interested in you as a person. They helped you to become the best that you could be, whatever that might be: not just achieving 'A's if you could, but growing as a whole person. We sensed that we were being educated in so many ways. We were lucky that the 'Fast Friends' programme started in our transition year: we named it.

The 'Fast Friends' programme is an example of a very broadening educational experience. It brings together our students and those with intellectual disabilities. Many people pass through life without getting that opportunity. All the social programmes help students to develop their skills in dealing with others, and their sense of what is right and standing up for what is right. It all builds towards the growth of responsible freedom, and the attitude of giving back, of thinking of the other person.

If the students are unkind I take the approach, 'How would that make *you* feel?' If they avoid answering I make them stay with the question, to try and bring the point home to them. I speak to them privately afterwards and make it clear that that is not how we do things here. *We do not say things like that, and we do not treat other people unkindly.* I give students the responsibility to treat each other well and the ability to recognise good ways of relating. In all my classes I try to bring out the qualities of kindness and respect.

All of the characteristics are founded on a strong belief system that Christ is behind them, and this is recognised. There are many faith activities, Mass at certain times, retreats, religious awareness, events for particular years. These are made available to students but are not forced on them. I think that people here feel a bit removed from the current criticism of the Church, because the Jesuits themselves are transparent in how they do things, they are 'with it', they are up for change, and you couldn't say that the Church as a whole is like that. They are good at spotting what needs to be changed and doing it. Here we are quite positive about change. That's a big thing.

There is hope in the way forward. I can see it in the classes I teach. The other day, after the second 'Fast Friends' meeting, we had a debriefing session. It was just amazing to see how the pupils are so into it, the way they have begun to relate to people from a different social background, with different ability levels. They are so caring, so respectful, so enthusiastic, so receptive and so connected with what we are trying to do – I was blown away. The school gives us the opportunity to do something like that.

Such opportunities allow them to 'fast forward' in learning life-skills; for example, not judging people, accepting others as they are, being men and women for God. That is the whole point of what we are trying to teach them – so that when they leave here they will have some sense of themselves, know right from wrong, and have a sense of faith. By and large, that's what our students are like when they leave, and wherever or whenever they meet up, all they talk about is the school! It's a frame of mind; it's a belief in God – without being holy. It's 'doing unto others…'; it's very special and you feel very lucky, very lucky indeed to have had this experience.

Cian Browne is a teacher of business, maths, social, personal and health education, and adults with special needs classes with transition year – and a past pupil – at Crescent College Comprehensive SJ.

RESPECTING DIVERSITY
Michael Clark

In a Jesuit school you are always questioning, and that is encouraged. Reason and faith can happily coexist. So for me, an attractive aspect of the Jesuit tradition is that there is no sense of conflict between the worlds of science and religion. The Jesuit approach is not one of regurgitating doctrine. Doctrine is respected; it is not imposed. It can be intellectually analysed, questioned and discussed without rancour.

A wide spectrum of religious views exists, certainly among the staff. You can talk and create dialogue without fear of repudiation or any sense of discord, whether the other be atheist or theist. It is important that students feel their intellectual understanding of faith can grow, just as their intellectual capacity in other subjects develops.

The religious menu offered is very wide, and ritual is important. Jesuit education has always valued the classical tradition, but it is forward looking too. You don't need to mention God specifically; you are assisting the development of your pupils' intellects, and are respectful of them and where they 'are at'. A well-developed mind is receptive to ideas. Maths and science have to go beyond the classroom – you need to speak to students' experience, and a subject has to be dynamic and relevant to gain their interest. The science classroom is a great environment to broaden their horizons and capture their imagination, if the subjects dealt with relate to their life experience. This creates an awareness of God in all things.

I have found that in Jesuit schools ethos is emphasised and interpreted in various ways. Some staff focus on the academic, and in particular academic rigour. I used to be of that school of thought myself. I suppose a subject like mathematics does favour those who are very able in that sphere, and this colours your view of students if you look at them purely through the prism of academic potential.

The academic and the child-centred approaches can co-exist quite happily. Both Gonzaga and Belvedere are orientated towards developing 'men for others'. In Belvedere the emphasis is on a 'child-centred' approach. Staff and pupils alike are expected to participate, or indeed immerse themselves, in co-curricular activities. A good working maxim is 'be prepared to do more'. The uniqueness and giftedness of pupils is more apparent to me through the co-curricular than in their academic performance. I also get a greater sense of the person outside the formal classroom setting, and a better grasp of their relationships with fellow students. Those who miss the boat at Belvedere are pupils who turn up for class but go home straight after school and avoid getting involved. I now appreciate that education in the fullest sense is about the whole person, including all their attributes and not only their academic progress.

This system means you have to be prepared to be involved. You cannot be peripheral – whether as a pupil, a parent or a staff member. You can expect students to challenge your views on religion. They have the confidence to expect you to enter into dialogue – even to engage in forensic dialogue – about matters of faith. They ask good questions, and you have the opportunity to defend your position and to take responsibility for your own belief. Students will stand up for themselves, but a core issue is to demonstrate consideration and respect: there is no question of imposing views.

I find the Jesuit Order fascinating and a bit enigmatic in relation to the Church. If I can use a football analogy – Jesuits are like the supporters of a football team, absolutely always behind the players, but well prepared to be critical of the management or the institution! Jesuits uphold the traditions of the Church, but within that there is a wide variation of beliefs and philosophical positions. Their approach is to be zealous and open to dialogue, with a willingness to engage actively on an intellectual battlefield, following the military discipline of Ignatius. Yet the Jesuit educational system is very respectful of diversity – it is a model very suited to modern Catholic education.

Michael Clark is a teacher of maths at Belvedere College SJ.

SUSPICIOUS OF EDUCATION
Bríd Dunne

On the first day of the higher diploma in education, an animated philosophy lecturer began his session by quoting the following letter:

Dear Teacher,

I am a survivor of a concentration camp. My eyes saw what no one should witness:

Gas chambers built by learned engineers;

Children poisoned by educated physicians;

Infants killed by trained nurses;

Women and babies shot and burned by high school and college graduates.

So, I am suspicious of education.

My request is: help your students to become more human. Your efforts must never produce learned monsters, skilled psychopaths, educated Eichmanns. Reading, writing and arithmetic are important only if they serve to make our children more human.

A poignant silence fell across the hundred students as we were asked to consider what our motivations were as teachers. 'Do you teach a subject or a child?' he asked. 'In a school or in a building?' 'For the greater good or for immediate success?' He went on: 'What are the main three reasons to be a teacher?' The suggested answer – 'June, July and August' – generated a relieving chuckle after the intensity of the previous reflections. But the question remained: what is our goal in the education of young people?

The letter above and this characteristic suggest that growth towards responsible freedom is central to lifelong education. Growth towards freedom acknowledges a meandering journey as fundamental. It is a process that suggests the expansion of mind and values towards an ultimate worth. This worth does not exist in isolation, but is connected deeply, on a human and spiritual level, to responsibility. Development education is a practical approach to growth towards responsible freedom. It is a sustained process of engaging young people in global issues in an active and tangible way. Through this process development education challenges the student's spirit to be moved towards action for social justice. Development education aims to encourage the fullness of human freedom and responsibility in our young people.

A number of years ago, I began to work with a fifth year class around the concept of global justice. This class was a relatively passive group. At one juncture during the term, the students were invited to assess a number of sentences and examine them in relation to the concepts of solidarity and charity. A continuum emerged across the class as the students articulated their standpoint in relation to the concepts. One question sparked an unprecedented debate in the group: *is running a pizza lunch fundraiser for a school in India an act of solidarity or of charity?*

From the ranks, one ordinarily docile student began to speak. She asked in a frustrated tone, 'why do we always have to benefit? The motivation seems to be for us to get something out of it. Why do we never do things just because they are the right thing to do, regardless of who is watching or waiting for a photo opportunity? We should do it because we can, because it's up to us, because it could be us, we should do it because we are all human.' There, in that fifth year classroom, was a group of students – and their teacher – gobsmacked by the content of that student's outpouring. There, in that fifth year classroom, growth in human freedom and responsibility was palpably in action.

Building an understanding of global justice in young people towards a growth in human freedom is a challenging phrase to read, let alone a process to begin. But it works, and therein lies the connection to the wider human family, to the kingdom of God. In educating our young people to be more human, to enjoy their blessings and use them for the common good, we partake in their growth towards responsible freedom.

Development education methodologies encourage students to develop their gifts and talents, to build their capacity for critical thinking, to respond to the world. It aids them to know themselves, to be fully human and to utilise their gifts to creatively demonstrate a genuine care for people they may never meet, simply because we are all human. It provides the tools to build towards connection with the wider human family on a deeper level, to be men and women for and with strangers! It is a process, reflective of the Ignatian vision for the world that is integral to supporting the human growth towards freedom and responsibility in our young people.

Bríd Dunne is a development education coordinator at the Irish Jesuit Mission Office.

GROWING TOWARDS FREEDOM AND RESPONSIBILITY
A conversation with Paul Kilraine

The characteristic that's particularly evident and valued in our school community is giving space for development and growth towards freedom and responsibility. This is a liberal school, less oppressive than some more traditional schools. Back in the 1970s it was a pioneer in abolishing corporal punishment. There is great freedom here to debate, and sometimes the liberal tag is applied to the school in a negative way. However, we find that because we encourage freedom of expression, our students are more mature on graduation and so are well prepared to make the transition to college life.

We focus very much on independent learning and the development of independence in transition year. We feel at this stage the students are ready for it. They get heavily involved as 'persons in the service of others' through social outreach activities. We expect them to make their own practical arrangements and to make their own way to locations: another approach that encourages independence. Social outreach challenges them to encounter their prejudices. They work with the marginalised, with asylum seekers and with people with disabilities. This helps them not to be totally self-absorbed. Debating is very strong, and we encourage them to run debating and sports activities themselves and to take leadership positions.

Our belief in Jesus Christ as a model underpins everything we do, but in a low-key way; it is not explicit. Mutual respect is a crucial value in the school culture, amongst students and between staff and students. They are quite gentle and low-key about it but they look out for each other and they will come and share their concerns. We assist them in building self-confidence. We have been told by staff in third-level colleges that they can identify our graduates – at their best they have a sense of freedom, of responsibility and a quiet confidence in themselves. Many who leave the school are not afraid to be different: they challenge things. They often get involved in activities that require dedication, maybe at a cost to themselves; and they care for each other.

Paul Kilraine is a teacher of chemistry, maths and science, and joint year head of the sixth year at Coláiste Iognáid SJ.

BETTER OFF WITHOUT ME?
Íde Tynan

St Ignatius placed great importance on educational institutions – for him they had an apostolic purpose, to bring about change and conversion. At St Declan's this process is at the very core of what we strive to do.

Each child comes with his or her own particular challenges which have reached the point when that child can no longer cope in a mainstream setting, despite the good intentions and often valiant efforts of parents, teachers and other health professionals. Fear of the unknown, lack of resources and skills, an inflexible and bureaucratic system have often resulted in the children being so overwhelmed and lacking in self-esteem that they have become locked in patterns of behaviour which are destructive, stifle their potential and only serve to reinforce their already negative self-image. They are convinced that they are worthless and that their parents – and everybody else –would be better off without them.

Our task, therefore, is to help them to come to love and accept themselves as they are, and to believe what is true: that they are made in the image and likeness of God and that they have much to offer this world, should they choose to fulfil their own unique potential.

This transformation doesn't happen easily or overnight. Just as our bodies experience growing pains, the growth required in order to change our negative beliefs about ourselves and patterns of behaviour can be a hard and rocky road with many backward steps along the way. Add to this the real challenges of developmental delays, specific learning difficulties and, sometimes, significant mental health issues and you get some inkling of just how hard these children have to struggle. *It's too hard, there's no point, I can't do it …* Such are the voices of fear that have to be overcome.

There are lots of tantrums, there are rewards and consequences, individual plans that have to be adjusted and readjusted, challenges that are set high enough to stretch but not so high that achievement is unrealistic. There are times when the struggle seems too much and children revert to old patterns, parents become frustrated and anxious, staff try one new approach after another without any visible progress – until suddenly a little breakthrough is made, and then another, and another, and you begin to see a light dawning in the child's eyes, you see their confidence grow and you sense the beginning of a real belief that he or she is genuinely a valued member of this community and does have something to offer.

Children have a canny way of cutting to the chase and asking the awkward questions that challenge us to question the status quo. It is incumbent on us to give these questions the respect and consideration they deserve. After all, didn't Jesus himself challenge us to see the world through the eyes of a child? When we begin to look at the world with the eyes of our children, we see many injustices that compel us to help them voice their experiences and advocate change.

Every day I have the privilege of witnessing wonderful children achieve this transformation for themselves and emerge more confident and assured of their worth as individuals, helped by the loving and guiding presence of parents, teachers, special needs assistants and other members of the school community.

St Declan's also offers a wonderful opportunity for growth for the adults who work with the children, and we too are often challenged to our very core. Sometimes just to carry on, remain patient and give continual encouragement when every helpful suggestion is met with resistance and often angry recrimination can require a huge effort. This effort can take its toll and requires a special kind of resilience yet, as Greg Boyle SJ says in his book *Tattoos on the Heart – The Power of Boundless Compassion*, 'Sometimes resilience arrives in the moment you discover your own unshakeable goodness'.[59]

As I write this I am picturing children's faces and hearing children's voices, and so it seems appropriate to end with a child's voice through his poem. I wonder if can I grow enough to live up to this challenge!

Use Your Heart!
by Daniel Rankin

Always love and always care
Help someone that's hurt and always share
Help your friends and always respect,
Don't tell lies – be honest
Don't get angry if you lose football
Don't just love yourself but love us all
Don't say bad words, say stuff that's kind,
Think of good deeds with your head and mind,
Be responsible – don't break things apart
That would mean you're not using your heart.

Íde Tynan is the principal of St Declan's Special NS, Dublin.

BECOMING LIKE CHRIST, FULLY HUMAN AND FULLY ALIVE

IDENTITY

The Jesuits are totally committed to Jesus Christ. Not to be so would be to turn our backs on what we call 'the Society or Company of *Jesus*'. We are not 'Ignatians', but 'companions of Jesus'. Our self-identity is summed up in a short phrase from a recent gathering of the Order: 'We know who we are by looking at him [Christ]'.[60] At the same time we respect the members of other faiths, and none, both staff and students. While we do not apologise for our beliefs, we do not proselytise. We defend the right to religious freedom, which 'has its foundation in the very dignity of the human person'.[61] We believe that by being true to ourselves and by giving an account of what motivates us, we can offer our best help to others. Plurality of beliefs can deepen the dialogue that accompanies the common search for truth.

Our starting place is our belief that human beings are made for God. As Hopkins says, 'Thee, God, I come from, to thee go'.[62] Therefore we facilitate students in entering a relationship with Jesus, God-made-human, so that they can accept his offer of companionship and friendship. Thus, they can come to be like him, fully human and fully alive. In the 1900s Friedrich von Hugel held that every important religion had three dimensions: the institutional, the intellectual and the mystical.[63] Each dimension is integral to the whole, and today we would add a fourth dimension, that missionary or evangelical outreach urged on every Catholic by Pope Francis in his 2013 exhortation, *The Joy of the Gospel*.[64] The Church in its *institutional* and *intellectual* levels is problematic for many good people today, including some of our students and their parents. But the *mystical dimension* is highly attractive in our time, as is evident from the huge interest in spirituality. This provides a natural starting point from which to introduce people to the Christian community. It respects the fact that at its core, Christianity is centred on relationships between the divine and the human, rather than on creeds and structures.

While young people may hold back from religious commitment for fear of entrapment, the invitation to a personal relationship with someone who respects and loves them is not threatening. Ignatius fell in love with the Jesus of the Gospels and helped others to do the same: we facilitate this experience for our students. Again, the emphasis is on *experience*. The experience of encounter with the Jesus of the Gospels precedes systematic engagement with the institutional and the intellectual dimensions of Christian faith, and has the potential to open students up to the fullness of life, which is another name for the divine. Our presentation of Jesus is tailored to the varying levels of experience of our student groups. Young people love life, friendship, sharing, exploring new horizons. Jesus offers them these experiences in abundance, as he did to his disciples. He presents himself as the liberating centre of their lives. We try to create an environment in which each can develop a personal relationship with him.

WHO IS JESUS?

Jesus is a member of the human race, fully human like ourselves, yet also unique. For us, nothing less than the affirmation of his divinity will do justice to this uniqueness. In Jesus we find God's self-portrait, the human face of God, which humankind longs to see. He reveals God as Pure Loving, committed to us and never holding anything against us. All our images of God are inadequate and have to be verified by comparison with that presented by Jesus.

And if he reveals God to us, he also reveals to us what it means to be fully human. In doing so he challenges us to examine our own, often hazy, presuppositions about what being human means. Students are fortunate to meet teachers who, in Patrick Kavanagh's lines, 'had the knack of making men feel as small as they really are/ which meant, as great as God had made them'.[65] When we think we know the measure of what it is to be human, we find that Jesus brings us further than we could ever dream. He is the exemplar of authentic humanity. Deep down, we wish to reach the fullness of our own reality. We yearn for the infinite without knowing what we are seeking, but he meets our yearning and transforms us – we become our true selves (John 1:12), boundlessly compassionate like himself, and fully alive.

As a human person Jesus responds totally to his Father's limitless concern for the world. He works to liberate us from all forms of domination, so that we can be free. He is wholly on our side (Romans 8:31–39) because he understands our human condition from within and accepts it, even to the point of dying as we do. But his dying is not simply an experience of mortality: he dies for us because he wants to liberate us from death itself. He is thus par excellence 'the Man for Others'. Students who have reached a certain level of self-transcendence and want to promote a more just world find in Jesus the support they need to continue in face of strong and strategic opposition. The Gospels come alive for them, as they sit with Jesus and ask him what kept him going in face of hostility and conflict. They come to know the dynamic of Jesus' suffering, death and resurrection in their own lives, and are strengthened to endure what might otherwise defeat them.

SCRIPTURE

A personal experience of recognising God in Jesus is at the heart of Christian faith. The Gospels offer a spectrum of encounters between Jesus and living characters with whom we can identify. These include Peter the fisherman, Matthew the tax-man and the other apostles; Nathaniel, who was sitting under a fig tree; Nicodemus, who showed up only at night; the Samaritan woman who met him accidentally at a well; the anonymous woman who was about to be stoned to death;

Martha and Mary, who provided much-needed hospitality for him, and so on. All are their unprecedented selves: some seem unlikely dialogue partners for Jesus, which gives hope to the rest of us!

Each encounter is direct, simple and seemingly accidental, but somehow things change for those who allow themselves to experience Jesus' loving and compelling presence. Each character feels known, loved and freed to walk in a new and richer way of life. This is how faith dawned on certain people, two thousand years ago. Today we try to facilitate such encounters with Christ in our pupils, and some respond. They find their deep-down needs met, and become, each in their own way, disciples of Jesus. They are on the road to becoming fully human and authentic themselves. This relationship with Christ is fostered by the Christian ethos of the school, and by offering meditation, prayer, retreats and the sacraments, together with service programmes, as constitutive components of the school's rhythm of life. As Pope Francis said in an address on 28 February, 2014: 'They must hear that Christ is not a character in a novel, but a living person, who wants to share their irrepressible desire for life, commitment, and dedication. If we content ourselves with offering them mere human comfort, we let them down.'

SUMMARY

Jesus is the human face of God because, like God, he loves us unrestrictedly.

He is the pattern of authentic humanity. Students become men and women for others through developing a life-giving personal relationship with Jesus.

The encounter with Jesus enables each person to feel known, loved, and freed to walk in a new and richer way of life.

This relationship with Christ is fostered by the Catholic ethos of the school.

Students are encouraged to participate in service programmes for the poor, which provide an experience of walking in companionship with Jesus, 'the Man for Others'.

Conscious of the spectrum of religious background in pupils and staff, we respect the freedom of each to engage or not in what is offered.

BECOMING LIKE CHRIST, FULLY HUMAN AND FULLY ALIVE

LIVING EXPERIENCE

LIVING EXPERIENCE

BUILDING A RELATIONSHIP WITH JESUS
Niamh O'Donoghue

When reflecting on the characteristic of Jesuit education that promotes Christ as the model for human life, I am struck by how counter-cultural this appears to be in today's world. As someone involved in faith formation in a Jesuit school I am ever conscious of the secular world that my students inhabit and of how other models of living are promoted much more successfully among young people than the Christian one. Such models often fly in the face of the Christian ideal. And yet, having learnt, experienced and taught Ignatian spirituality, I am at ease in knowing that this characteristic provides precisely the approach that students need. It allows great personal freedom, acknowledges the challenges of faith in today's world and invites each person to develop in his or her own way a personal relationship with Jesus Christ.

In a society where subjectivity seems to be the order of the day, and where the focus is so often inward rather than on the needs of others, the image of the person of Jesus could appear to some to be a 'hard sell', given the selfless nature of the life that he lived. However, in my experience, young people have a far greater depth than they are given credit for; when they are given the space, freedom and experiences to come to know Jesus, the vast majority recognise the value of trying to live that way. The greatest obstacle to achieving this is not the person of Jesus himself, but their disconnection from the institution of the Church and their alienation from the idea of organised religion.

Ignatian educators, in my experience, are encouraged to think 'outside the box' as they seek ways to bring the person of Jesus before their students. The greatest challenge is to help students take the first step in building a relationship with him, and so they need to *experience* what Christian faith means, to witness a faith *in action*, rather than learning about it from a textbook. Some will find God on O'Connell Bridge in the person of a homeless man whom they meet on the soup run. They may see him in the eyes of a child in the slums of Kolkata, feel his presence around the cross at Taizé on Holy Saturday night or in the sharing of peer stories and experiences on a Kairos retreat. They may find him in the kind words of a chaplain, in the support of a prefect or in the silence of their Examen prayer. Others may see him in the caring nurse on the wards in Lourdes or in the faces of those working with people on the margins of our society. Ignatian spirituality allows us to see Christianity as an active way of living rather than a daunting rulebook removed from the real world in which we live.

When we support our students as they make the link between what they believe and how they live, they begin to ask more searching questions about the person of Jesus. What they find is the epitome of what a 'man for others' should be. They find that the only rules are compassion, forgiveness, tolerance, acceptance, unconditional love and a respect for the dignity of every human being. They find a man who flew in the face of authority when it was needed, who welcomed all who asked for help, who led others to a better way of life and who demanded that social justice be lived rather than simply believed. Yet, in the midst of all of this, they find a man who was strikingly alive, not someone reluctantly serving others in the hope of reward; a man who shared meals with friends, who lived in deep relationship with so many different types of people and, most of all, a man who chose not to conform to an unjust *status quo*, but to follow his own path even in the face of persecution. They wish to be like him. The result is so often an attraction to the person of Jesus and a challenge to every one of them to strive to be the best version of themselves that they can, secure in the knowledge that if Jesus Christ is the self-portrait of God, forgiveness is indeed a given when they fail.

The challenge to us as educators is to find ways to create the space for students to hear the invitation to relationship with the person of Jesus Christ, to hit the 'pause button' long enough for him to be heard. We want them to realise we are fully alive as human beings when we live the way he taught. Even with the challenges facing our faith in the world today, we cannot but respond with love when we come to realise that we are loved unconditionally. Our job as teachers is to help our students, in the midst of their crazy world, to 'tune in' and to allow God to be heard.

Niamh O'Donoghue is a teacher of religious education, history and social, personal and health education at Belvedere College SJ.

CHALLENGING DARKNESS AND TRAGEDY
A conversation with Eileen O'Donohoe

Teachers in the Ignatian tradition are only too aware that its characteristics are ideals to strive for. When we don't reach them we should not feel negative, though it can be difficult to avoid this. I need to think of the characteristics as open to interpretation and development to suit different times and places: they are dynamic.

In the school we take Christ as our role model. This is a demanding ideal. In following him we do not expect to be perfect. We are allowed to fail, but always with the hope of continuing. Hope is an important part of all of this. For followers of Christ, forgiveness is central, and this includes forgiveness of ourselves and of others. Loving your neighbour is not easy. There are the daily tensions and conflicting agendas; we experience disappointment and hurt. But in rising above these painful realities we encounter real hope. This is where resurrection and redemption occur in everyday life. I feel that if parents and teachers can key into this message, it is a great basis for true friendship with young people. We need to find a way to help them deal with conflict and disappointment *in a way that encourages them*. It is through our hope in Christ that we can challenge darkness and tragedy.

We help them best through meaningful conversation. In times of darkness, this shared space where they can talk allows them to draw strength from each other. They feel that they can reach out for something bigger than themselves. It is so important for us to find ways of challenging the current culture of risky behaviour, of low self-esteem, of relationship difficulties, of unmitigated hopelessness.

Most staff feel that the most accessible characteristic is *cura personalis*, or care of the person. All are attracted to it, as they

98

genuinely care for their students. It is a very live concern in school life. For example, if a policy is being changed, the yardstick against which it is judged is always 'will this add to the care of the person?' This is the characteristic that encourages many to get heavily involved in running the co-curricular programmes in the school.

It also inspires the work of special needs education. Once you believe in the individual, you focus on what his or her exact learning needs are. You find ways to break things down into small accessible chunks. You encourage students to see that you have high expectations of them, and you encourage parents to see the strengths rather than the limitations of their child. In special education being 'a person for others' encourages cooperative learning, and we find that working with others can be of great benefit to all. So this value informs the way we work within Special Needs, and also influences the social outreach activities in the school.

Above all, we develop a sense that we are being divinely led. Ignatius spoke of us becoming co-creators with God in our work. Through our focus and reflection on these values we are taken somewhere new, and we need to hold on to that energy. The characteristics are a framework of ideas – a scaffolding that enables us to grow. They allow us to engage in discovery, and sometimes bring us to an entirely new place.

If we are overburdened, we can focus too much on what we are not doing, or not getting around to. Maybe we need to look more at what we *are* doing. There are lots of wonderful moments where we are. I find images very potent: they often stay with you longer than a theory or words. My image of *cura personalis* is that of holding a child. If you really hold a child, he or she feels loved, safe and secure, even in the midst of turmoil. That is what we try to become for them – a secure place where they are valued and where they can grow to their full potential.

Eileen O'Donohoe is the coordinator of Ignatian ethos and a special education needs teacher at Coláiste Iognáid SJ.

UNTIL YOU BROUGHT JESUS IN
A conversation with Anita O'Shea

The care of the person is the characteristic that I would really emphasise. From it everything else flows. Whether in the classroom, or in the boarding house or on the rugby pitch, whether you are doing drama or taking the students away on a trip, you are responsible for them and you want them to be at their best That is why we provide so many activities for them. Care for the person helps define our relationships with our students: these are characterised by being very warm, respectful (in the main!), familial, indeed especially here, given the nature of our particular school. This year I am assistant year head for the second years and, as I was telling them that they were my group and that I would be working with them, I was immediately described as a 'Mammy teacher' or the 'go-to person' for everything.

The religious element, being energised by the example of Christ, can be challenging. I did meditation with a class one day and thought it went really well, but as they left one lad said 'that was good, Miss, until you brought Jesus into it'. So I was left wondering what we need to do to get over that hurdle! It *is* a challenge to communicate that dimension, whereas they will accept 'being a person for others'. The social justice elements of the characteristics get the most enthusiasm: fasting, fund-raising and fun. But often they don't go beyond that to the more reflective side of things: they buy in on different levels.

Excellence is now interpreted in terms of the person rather than by external standards, so we want each of our students to be the best that he can be. This also includes the 'bread and butter' academic issues, which influences our approach to teaching and our work in the classroom. We stretch them academically so that they grow and develop through the six-year cycle. We see them change and mature and develop as people. That's a privileged vantage point for us as teachers.

There is a dichotomy between trying to educate and getting leaving certificate points! We want them to develop as persons for others, but their exam performance is important too. Some parents are fixated on academic results – I am frequently asked, 'can you guarantee my son an "A" in the leaving certificate?'. You can't guarantee anything, but you do have to help them to achieve to their ability. We live in the real world!

We have a mixed intake and there is very strong learning support for those who need it. That has to be factored in too. It can provide an opportunity for some to work on homework together, so they are aware of supporting each other. We also run competitions and programmes that target and encourage gifted children as well: there is a maths modelling programme with University of Limerick and academic writing competitions run between the schools, such as the Beckett and Joyce awards.

Ours is a model that works: people do embrace it. Recent research in relation to ethos and the characteristics among past pupils and parents showed that they recognised the qualities and values of our educational system. It is well understood that we do things for a reason, and that the reason is based on our religious perspective. However, it is important also to say that there is great respect for the personal religious position of each individual. There is participation from parents, who are now more involved in the school through the Parents' Association. They know we are serving the community and the Church, and that we are operating from a faith perspective.

Anita O'Shea is a teacher of English and religion at Clongowes Wood College SJ.

COMMUNICATING VALUES
Catherine Scannell

The mention of Christ in any conversation can meet with resistance. Hence the frequent warning, 'Never discuss religion and politics at dinner'!

More than ten years ago our school was rebranded as 'Crescent College Comprehensive SJ'. We describe ourselves as 'A Catholic Comprehensive in the Jesuit tradition'. The context of the rebranding involved certain changes in society and a shift in attitude to the Church and religious orders. At that time, for instance, we had a teacher in the school who was very dismissive, I believe, of what he called the 'God Stuff'. There can be tension here between 'believer' and 'non-believer'.

A couple of years ago I was on a family holiday: we found ourselves one evening walking along a jetty near the harbour. The jetty stretched for about a mile out into the ocean. All along one wall there were lines of fishermen active at their task. On our return, they had all gone, but as I was walking by I noticed several memorial plaques along the wall. The messages were very similar: *'Joe Bloggs, age 56, gone fishing on 4th March 2006'.* My interpretation was that this revealed a secular approach to death: that Joe Bloggs would have seen that fishing trip as his last journey, which was not followed by another. For him it was the end: there was no life hereafter.

I think this story might have relevance for a number of us today- the conflict between belief and non-belief touches us all. Some might say, 'Well, I don't believe either – I am of the *Gone Fishing* variety'. But the theme of Christ is central to Jesuit education.

Does this make me an ineffective teacher? Or an ineffective educator? A less understanding teacher? I believe not. The educational community in Jesuit schools can share the conviction that the story of Jesus has characteristics that enriches our profession.

If we look at the model of Christ *what* are his ways of behaviour? What values are being modelled? I believe they include: Compassion; Tolerance; Service; Inclusiveness; Respect; Acceptance; Justice; Love.

It is my contention that it is our *behaviour* that matters more than our belief – how we interact with students and among ourselves as staff. 'It is by our *actions* that we know we are living in the truth' (1 John 3:18-19).

I invite you to focus on a 1st year student who has arrived here in the school this year. I believe we all have a vision for that child. While focussing on your own beliefs, try to see what values you want to transfer to the child.

Taking those three elements, the child, your values, your beliefs, I invite you to go on a journey with that child and arrive here six years on, on Graduation night. What do you want for that young adult?

I believe that the vision we all have for the twelve-year-old student who comes through our doors for the first time is shared right across the staff, whether we see ourselves as believers or non-believers. We want to form every student so as to enable them to choose their best path to a meaningful life. We want our pupils to graduate as persons who believe in their own self-worth; who acknowledge the value of each individual; who will heighten rather than diminish human lives by becoming men and women of competence, conscience and compassion.

I believe we pass on these values both in our teaching and non-teaching. The Business suite of subjects for example consistently offers situations that require value judgements: profit versus exploitation; child labour; sweat shops; etc. Or the ethics of the national Budget – where should the axe fall when cuts have to be made?

Teaching any subject requires value judgements. In your own subject area, what values do you pass on? You are the only adult in the classroom, so how you *practise* those values is under the spotlight. In my research, I came across a quote that states 'Values are not taught, but *caught and practised*'. We are always under scrutiny. Our actions, reactions, words are constantly being analysed by the students. Theory is one thing; practice and behaviour quite another. How we behave in all aspects of school life reflects on our commitment to inculcating values in our students.

For this contribution I asked colleagues for some insights. I was advised to get a few supportive quotes from Ignatius of Loyola, but I opt to quote Dudley Herbert instead. On the topic of ethos, which I define as 'how we do things around here', Dudley had a mantra: 'Ethos is in the classrooms and corridors around here, not in the books'. How we treat the students is what matters. Ethos is concretised in the lived-out experiences of all our daily interactions with the students. The example we give is what the student sees.

Another colleague relayed the story of Kathleen Kennedy. She was teaching a teenager with a reading age of about six, who was coming from a socially disadvantaged background. Both academic progress and behaviour were challenging. Our colleague enquired of Kathleen: 'Well, what do you do in that situation?' And Kathleen replied, 'Sure all you can do is love them'.

On the spectrum of belief here, some of us may place ourselves in the *'Gone Fishing'* school of thought, while others of us see our destiny in the *'Kingdom of God'*. But however we classify ourselves, it is my contention that the values and behavioural characteristics of Jesus can enrich all our lives.

Catherine Scannell teaches Business Studies and Accounting at Crescent College Comprehensive SJ.

WALKING THE WALK: CHRIST AS ROLE MODEL
Jerry Sheehan

When contemplating this characteristic I instantly refer back to the human qualities and attributes of Jesus. Trying to bring this characteristic to life and incorporate it into your everyday life can be quite challenging, but very rewarding. As religion teachers and chaplains in a Jesuit school, we always strive to provide pupils with solid and valuable experiences of Catholic prayer, Catholic faith and a Catholic spirituality. It is here where I always think of Jesus' encounter with the disciples on the road to Emmaus. As religious educators, it is our responsibility to help pupils recognise the presence of Jesus in their lives. This can be done through retreats, services, pilgrimages, outreach programmes etc. However it's our one-to-one relationship with every pupil that really has a lasting effect. This involves showing genuine compassion and concern for the individual, allowing for mistakes and encouraging them to show their best qualities.

In the everyday bustle of school life teachers and chaplains are met with a range of demanding situations – deadlines, discontented staff, discontented pupils, discontented parents – and it is easy to get caught up in all the stress that difficulties can bring. This is where Jesus' calming of the storm always comes to my mind. Jesus showed qualities of trust, courage, calmness and confidence in this miracle. To be calm and to trust that Jesus will come to your aid provides an invaluable way of approaching the thorny situations each day can throw up. As people of faith it is important that we show these qualities as Christ did in all aspects of his life.

Throughout his life, Jesus preached about the Kingdom of God. In an unjust society of homelessness, poverty, drug addiction and so on, the Kingdom can easily be overlooked. Christ encourages us to be active Catholics who show love, compassion, care and support for those in need. This can easily be achieved by involving ourselves in social justice projects and encouraging others to make the same commitment. To put it in lay terms: we can talk the talk but now we have to walk the walk. Strong role models can help others: staff, parents and pupils realise the importance of being active Christians.

There are times in your life, be it at school, at home or in social life, when you find yourself having to stand up for your faith. This can lead to disagreements, broken friendships and, in general, awkward situations. Being a Christian in the twenty-first century is not a popular vocation for most. Our religion, our faith, is something that has to be protected, but also made appealing. Be it in religion class, in the staff room or at home, we are representatives of Christ's message. As Catholics it is important to bring to life the Gospel values that Jesus preached. This can only be done through building a relationship with Jesus. Therefore, as chaplains and religious educators we should encourage people to develop such a relationship. We can do this through prayer, the daily Examen of Consciousness, meditation and other practices.

Christ encouraged inclusiveness, respect, honesty, courage, trust, love and compassion. These attributes can be promoted in every challenge we take on at school and at home. But this is a lot easier said than done. The world we live in can often thrive on negativity, jealousy and unhealthy competitiveness; it is a world where social media dictates the agenda and fuels the primary importance of a good self-image. It is easy to get caught up in it all. It is therefore important to try to trust and develop Christ's message and values. We are challenged to embrace the Gospel and bring it to life.

Jerry Sheehan is the chaplain at Coláiste Iognáid SJ.

ARTISANS OF A NEW HUMANITY ...
A FAITH THAT DOES JUSTICE

The characteristics of Jesuit education illuminate one another. Thus, the quest for truth involves searching for the presence of God in a distorted world where more than half of the population lives below the poverty level. One billion of these are children, of whom 22,000 die daily from diseases linked to poverty.[66] Finding God in the voices of the poor and the dominated requires a developed social conscience and a sensitive engagement with victims. Responsible use of freedom makes God present in situations of injustice. Vatican II speaks of the emergence of a new generation of men and women who will be the 'artisans of a new humanity'.[67] We want our alumni to be among them.

THE PROMOTION OF JUSTICE

Vatican II, 1962–1965, brought the Church out of a self-chosen isolation from the world. The Church had viewed itself as a 'perfect society', which kept itself uncontaminated by the sordid realities of human life. Then came the Pastoral Constitution, *The Church in the Modern World*, with its revolutionary opening statement: 'The joys and hopes, the grief and anguish of the people of our time, especially of those who are poor or afflicted, are the joys and hopes, the grief and anguish of the followers of Christ as well.'[68]

But how could the Christian community make this aspiration real? In 1971 a short but powerful Roman document, titled 'Justice in the World', said that faith and justice must always go together.[69] In a sense there was nothing new in this: it was rather the retrieval of a long tradition. The God of the Hebrews is a liberating God, who hears the cry of the poor; the voice of victims is the voice of God (see Exodus 3:7). And in the fullness of time, Jesus is sent to bring good news to the poor and the victims of injustice. While the Church had always been in the forefront of charitable activity, now the very *structures of injustice* were to be challenged.

Pedro Arrupe, Superior General of the Order from 1965 to 1983, offended many Jesuit alumni when, in 1973, he challenged them to become 'men for others'. Perhaps he was asking too much too soon? The Order itself, not without inner resistance, committed itself to this direction in 1974, in a decree titled *'Our Mission Today: The Service of Faith and the Promotion of Justice'.*[70] Every ministry and resource was to be evaluated in relation to it. It was a challenging and confusing time. Jesuits queried, in all sincerity, *how can a school or a theology faculty become an agent of justice in the world*? Others considered that our prestigious institutions were fostering inequality rather than diminishing it, by creating social divisions. Another group argued that a disincarnate spirituality, focused on 'heavenly things, not on the things that are on the earth' (Colossians 3:2), had to be abandoned in favour of the promotion of a 'new heavens and earth' *within human history*.

The high ideals embedded in promoting faith and justice as a unit were painful to implement. They led to deep divisions, but also to heroism. Some Jesuits threw themselves into the struggle for justice so deeply that they seemed to ignore the promotion of faith, which was integral to the new orientation. Nearly fifty Jesuits were killed in the service of the poor between 1974 and 2014. Most notable were the six men who defied the Salvadorean authorities by defending the poor, and paid the ultimate price, together with two women, in 1989.

MEN AND WOMEN FOR AND WITH OTHERS

Our colleges undertook a massive internal transformation. Despite the need for Jesuits on the front line of social justice, the Society reaffirmed the importance of its educational apostolate, but this was now charged with the task of an integral promotion of faith and justice. Within the slogan, 'men and women for others' the word *for* is loaded with meaning. It asks students to be positive toward others open, inclusive, interested, wanting their good and helping them to achieve it. It moves beyond an intellectual openness to strong commitment – it entails a willingness to go the extra mile and to act as advocates for those who cannot help themselves. It means making difficult decisions in order to help the needy. While all pupils have to get a job, perhaps enter professional life, become specialists or entrepreneurs, the ideal of being *for* others must find expression in whatever milieu they choose.

The personal care and respect that students receive must be shared with others less fortunate. Being *for* others is the height of human achievement – the exemplar is Jesus who is wholly *for* us all, and who thus reveals what it means to be fully human. To be Christian is 'to live the same kind of life as Christ lived' (1 John 2:6). He is *with us* through his becoming human, and he is *for us* to the limit. 'A man can have no greater love than to lay down his life *for* his friends' (John 15:13). This fifth characteristic reminds us of the height of our Christian vocation. Experiences of involvement with the poor are offered to all students. We are to be in solidarity with the poor, not simply helping them from a secure distance. Always a work in progress, the task of providing a justice energised by faith is central to the ethos of Jesuit schooling. Our schools in their various dimensions are to be an embodiment of faith and justice.

WITNESSES TO ALTRUISM

We are talking about Christian altruism, and it is learnt by example. The witness of parents carries great weight, so this is an important challenge for them, because students need parental support. The dedication of teaching staff to their pupils, and the orientation towards justice in the structures and atmosphere of a school, are essential. Instances of altruism can be found in the sacrifices made to fund bursaries and scholarships so that the less fortunate may be able to access Jesuit education. *Fe y Alegria*, a project begun by the Jesuits in Venezuela in 1955, is a movement for integral popular education and social development, whose activities are directed to the most impoverished and excluded sectors of the population. The goal is to empower them in their personal development and their participation in society. *Fe y Alegria* flourishes in 16 countries, especially in Latin America, and touches millions of people who have no other access to education. Such initiatives are practical instances of faith doing justice.

Christians have no monopoly on altruism! God searches out good hearts everywhere and urges them to donate themselves to the good of others. Malala Yousafzi, a Pakistani teenager, and now the youngest ever Nobel Prize laureate, was shot in the head when the Taliban attacked a school bus. This was 2012. When she recovered, she addressed the UN Youth Delegates on the fight for universal education. 'Let us pick up our books and our pens. They are our most powerful weapons. One child, one teacher, one book, and one pen can change the world. Education is the only solution.'[71]

SUMMARY

The search for truth involves searching for God in a distorted world where more than half of the population lives below the poverty level.

Jesuits are fundamentally orientated towards the service of faith and the promotion of justice.

'Men and women for and with others' summarises the values and goal of Jesuit education.

Jesuit alumni are challenged to put their educational and socio-economic opportunities at the service of those in need. People of conscience, they are to be willing to stand for truth and be advocates for the voiceless.

While religious conviction is deeply personal, it cannot be privatised.

Faith lacks authenticity if it does not emerge in a passion for justice. 'Love ought to find expression in deeds rather than in words.' (*Spiritual Exercises* n.230)

TEN FACTS ABOUT GLOBAL POVERTY

1. 80% of the world population live on less than $10 a day. Nearly half of the world's population – more than 3 billion people – live on less than $2.50 a day. Half of these again live in extreme poverty, that's on less than $1.25 a day.
2. 1 billion children are living in poverty. According to UNICEF, poverty kills 22,000 children each day.
3. More than 1 billion people lack clean drinking water and an estimated 400 million of these are children. Because unclean water breeds illness, roughly 443 million school days are missed every year.
4. In 2011, 165 million children under the age of five were stunted owing to chronic malnutrition.
5. 870 million people worldwide do not have enough food to eat.
6. Preventable diseases such as diarrhoea and pneumonia take the lives of 2 million children per year.
7. As of 2011, 19 million children worldwide are not vaccinated.
8. A quarter of all humans live without electricity – approximately 1.6 billion.
9. In 1998, the UN estimated that it would take $58 billion annually to offer basic education, clean water and sanitation, reproductive health, and basic health and nutrition to every person in every developing country.
10. The World Food Programme says, 'The poor are hungry and their hunger traps them in poverty'. Hunger is the number one cause of death in the world, killing more than HIV/AIDS, malaria and tuberculosis combined.[72]

ARTISANS OF A NEW HUMANITY: FAITH THAT DOES JUSTICE

LIVING EXPERIENCE

LIVING EXPERIENCE

THE DOING OF JUSTICE

Anonymous

My engagement with the fifth characteristic began as a result of having to deal with the daily reality of being just one of a group of young teachers in classrooms with teenagers, trying to find ways to help them make sense of the distorted world that their critical eyes revealed. The struggle was, for me, an endless source of deep frustration and failure. The teenagers believed that if there was no justice there was no truth. If there was no truth there could be no faith. Even more importantly, if there was no evidence of a concrete and tangible response to 'the voices of the poor', then all the theory and fine rhetoric that they were used to hearing was relegated to the wastelands of hypocrisy, and simply confirmed their analysis that their world was indeed fundamentally a distorted world, a world where faith was meaningless, a world where there could be no God. Their challenge to us was always a very simple demand to prove that things were otherwise!

An encounter with Arrupe's 'Men for Others' was a revelation in terms of the simplicity, clarity and undeniable truth that is at the centre of the challenge to make real 'a Faith that Does Justice'. In the classroom the critical aspect of Arrupe's challenge was centred on the word 'does'. If there was an unequivocal, open and honest effort to connect with those suffering injustice, then a portal opened up through which those teenagers had the real possibility of finding God in the practical responses we could make to the needs of the Poor. Everything hung on the doing of justice.

So we had to find ways to reach out and be with the poor. This demanded personal investment. One of the great strengths of those teenagers was their unequivocal willingness to 'go the extra mile'; this tapped into their innate respect for the hero and the call to heroism that Arrupe demanded. Our collective understanding of the fifth characteristic was unambiguous: there was no questioning it. It was for them a statement of the obvious. Quite simply, it was right, true, honest. They believed in its power to re-order the world, and make justice in society attainable. They willingly stepped through the portal that the fifth characteristic opened up before us.

The values embedded in it began to be practised. They began to seep into daily life on the corridors of the school, into the fabric of the classrooms. They extended out to the families and the wider community. Our experience, over a very long period of time, has been profound. In this vibrant school community I have seen several million euros raised by enthusiastic teenagers from thirteen through to eighteen on behalf of a wide range of people in need. They have walked the length and breadth of Ireland, climbed mountains, cycled thousands of kilometres, reached out on behalf of those who suffer from the distortions in our local, national and international communities. They have held hands with the young and old, sat down on the ground and simply been with the lost and alienated of our society. They have reached out to be with the sick, those suffering disabilities and challenges. They have had the courage and compassion to allow themselves to be with people who endure the most appalling pain and degradation. They have sat quietly and prayerfully with people in the last moments of their lives. I have been blessed to have been in the company of heroes. Their instinctive altruism has created experiences through which subsequent year groups have learnt by example.

On Christmas Eve of 2013 I stood opposite the Dublin General Post Office, where there was a large group of secondary school students fasting and sleeping out on behalf of Focus Ireland and The Fr Peter McVerry Trust. I smiled privately. I continued on up towards the Bank of Ireland, to find another group of young men, past pupils doing another sleep-out. No one had ever asked past pupils to do this. No one had ever tried to motivate them or encourage them. They were inspired by their experiences as schoolboys and, as young men, decided to initiate another effort to support the homeless people of Dublin. Nearly thirty years later and the fifth characteristic was still leading them!

I worked my way around the city streets and came upon a group of past and current pupils as they slipped into an anonymous building that was in the middle of renovation work. They had got the permission of the owner to make it their base to store supplies that would be delivered to the homeless on the city streets. They were continuing to bring the fifth characteristic to life. At the core of this group were young men who had been taught some of life's greatest lessons by the finest teachers on the planet – the poor and destitute, the sick, suffering and dying, and the street children of Kolkata. Being with people during some of the most difficult times of their lives is a blessing. While trying to be there for them, one of the great mysteries unfolds. As Hopkins described it in 'Felix Randal', 'this seeing the sick endears them to us, us too it endears'.[73] I have witnessed the most dramatic and powerful experiences when young men's lives are transformed by being with the poor.

Such a young man, recently arrived in Kolkata and exasperated by the suffering around him, wept and sighed, 'Where is God in all of this?' There was real despair and hopelessness in his voice. There seemed to be no God in this distorted world. His friends sobbed gently, too, at the magnitude of suffering all around. There was a deep silence in the room, awaiting an authoritative voice to offer some theological insight. None was to be heard! No one rushed in with answers in an effort to rebuild the shattered faith of this young man. He was simply asked to live as best he could with the children he came to be with, with the people of Kalikat, Mother Teresa's home for the sick and dying, and the residents of Titigarh, a community where people with leprosy live. Shortly before we left Kolkata we returned and put his own question to him, 'Where is God in all of this?' The silence returned and the room was filled with an expectant tension. What had he been taught by the people he had been with, we wondered? His answer was clear, unequivocal and profound. He simply smiled and said 'Everywhere!' Without realising it, he had lived through and explored the reality of Matthew 25:35-40; it had spoken to him.

The greatest obstacle to the 'work of justice' is our own ego. When we seek recognition for our efforts, even when we tell the stories of the poorest of the poor, we in fact rob them of their dignity all over again. Their story belongs to them and is not ours to give away. Hence I have tried very hard not to retell their personal stories here. That is why I have asked for my name to be withheld, as it doesn't matter who I am, and should be of no interest to anyone. The truth is that I am just one of a group of teachers who have helped students find the space from which they could make their own journey into the mystery of faith and belief, guided by the wisdom of the fifth characteristic, which truly is a portal for God's love to become tangible, real, credible and concrete.

The author teaches at an Irish Jesuit College.

BRING THE LORD WITH YOU
A conversation with Ann Cooke

The idea of inspiring the boys to be 'men for others' is very important here. For example, the students get the opportunity to work outside the school with others, and it's brilliant how they do it. Also, if there is a discipline issue, it becomes a learning opportunity, as it is built around showing them a better way to do things, how to make better choices. Discipline is always about doing things for others. The head of boarding will always tell the boys, 'bring the Lord with you and don't just have him up on the cross'. The staff leads by example. The Jesuits give an amazing example to the boys. The prayer of St Ignatius is all around the place, and it really inspires people. Even if you don't feel like doing something, that prayer makes you go back and get on with it! It inspires on a daily basis.

People here are treated exceptionally well; it is a great environment. I worked for many years in the catering business and in hotels at a senior level, and here it's so different – it's much more personal, a much better work environment. The Jesuits treat workers well, more so than people may appreciate. They treat you like family. Anywhere else, everyone has their day-to-day work, and you can have a bad day. But here everyone greets you, and it is not hard to be cheerful; it lifts you. We help each other in this way. The boys are so genuinely nice; I find that through working here I have a much better appreciation of young people.

The boys love to come back after the breaks. They are very well supported by the care structure – the prefects and the year heads, who don't just stay in their offices but are out mingling with the boys. The care of the person here is a very strong value. When the first years arrive, they are given close attention to ensure that they are eating well, as there can be a period of adjustment to being away from home, and the staff are very mindful of that.

Things are done in a quiet way, without big drama. The school is run like their home; the Jesuit way is quite low key. Many people coming here have their roots in Christian belief and spirituality. Here those roots can find soil; it feels like coming home. God is in your life. The other day, passing the petrol station, I saw a lady trip, and a few of our boys were nearby and they immediately ran to help. Some other boys nearby jeered at them, but I could not but be struck by their reaction; it is part of what they are to be concerned for others.

The day starts with Morning Prayer and gives a sense of God to the day. I led the prayer recently, and I gave them a little lesson on how the Church in the past had to be prepared to fight for the faith – I knew the idea of fighting would catch the boys' attention! The faith thing is more personal here. At my boarding school our faith was more routine, more of a ritual. Here, at night-time, if you pop into the chapel there are boys there, and not always the ones you would expect! When a member of the Jesuit community died there was a vigil here, and the boys were able to stay and pay their respects to him. The retreats each year can be an amazing experience for them; it helps them to share and to bond, and sometimes to get to know the boys from other classes.

I think that they are offered a chance to see the *joy* in faith; it is not all about the death on the cross. If someone has done something wrong the staff try to show him that what was done was not in line with being a 'man for others' and the correction will develop a sense of responsibility. They are treated like young men; they are taught that if they have been blessed with opportunity, then they also have added responsibility.

The staff and Jesuits work very hard to deliver the quality of care that the boys experience. This is not easy; it takes constant effort and long hours to do what is being done here. Hard work is appreciated: the only danger is that you could become a workaholic, but I think we avoid that! I would put kindness in the care of others very high on the list of priorities here. This gives the boys a good sense of how to be a 'person for others' in small ways.

Ann Cooke is the catering manager at Clongowes Wood College SJ.

SLÍ EILE SOUTH AFRICA TRIP
Darragh Leonard

Some years ago a group of students, teachers and I travelled to South Africa to engage in volunteer work, a mixture of teaching and building. The group was divided into two sub-groups of nine, one to further the building of a four-classroom complex at a school, the other to construct its toilet block.

The poverty of the area was extreme. The life expectancy for a man in this province is 44 years; neither electricity nor running water is available to the majority. The prevalence of AIDS is estimated at 60 per cent. Many children, some of whom walked up to 15 kilometres to school, had no footwear. Food is at a premium and the children on site received a government-aided lunch of a piece of loaf and water sourced from a nearby stagnant pond. The local workers, who were paid 5–10 euros per day, would not eat anything from 8.00 in the morning to 6.00 in the evening. The toilets were no more than corrugated out-houses without running water or privacy.

But even though materially they had nothing, the people had something that many Irish people have lost: happiness and contentment with their situation. People there seemed to take a huge amount from their sense of community. Relationships defined their lives and they devoted much of their time to them. Neighbours saw and talked to each other many times daily and were bound together by the common purpose of survival. Collecting food and water were community activities. Any excess was shared, any hardships were halved and any good fortune was divided up. The pursuit of material things was not an issue: having enough to survive was. Our group learnt a lot from this; particularly in terms of humility and an appreciation of the lives and comforts we take for granted every day.

Throughout our stay we developed relationships with the local site and school workers, the children, and indeed with each other. One of the first things that struck us was that when we were greeted each morning or bade farewell each evening it was done with vigour and in a way that meant something. There wasn't a quick hello as they walked by, but a concerned 'how are you?' accompanied by a handshake, smile and open body language.

One of the greatest rewards was in becoming friends with the other members of the group. We were bound by a common purpose and linked by shared experience along the way. Not only did we have common experiences, but we shared our perspectives on them in rewarding reflective exercises. These young people will remain in my life, and I wonder, were it not for the trip, would I ever have talked to them again? ... Probably not.

Another theme that ran through the trip for me was that of trust. Fifteen short years earlier, apartheid rule was in place throughout South Africa. With this in mind the acceptance we were met with was astounding. The welcomes were as many as there were people by the roadside: young and old never failed to wave as we passed by.

As the trust developed between us and the local workers, I learnt their values; acceptance, trust, unselfishness, patience, appreciation and cooperation. One of our achievements was to foster trust between black and white on this local scale and, perhaps, to initiate a ripple effect into the wider community. For the locals to sit and eat with us, ask our opinions about the project and tell us about *their* hopes and plans for life and beyond was amazing. They truly shared their innermost feelings and concerns. Sharing at this level showed how far their trust had developed.

Also evident every day was the spirituality of the local people. This was exemplified by the three-and-three-quarter-hour Mass we attended. For them it was a social occasion and the highlight of their week, a celebration not only of their faith, but of all the things that are good in their lives. Though the Mass celebration was a most obvious symbol of the spirituality, it was also evident throughout their daily activities. Living and acting in a Christian way is the most spiritual thing of all. We saw how much they cared for their neighbours. This experience led to something of a spiritual awakening in some members of the group. Also, seeing the happiness and contentment of the locals with so few resources could not fail to make us think. Reflection is a process in which we rarely engage, but we practised it daily in Africa. I gained much, not only from reflecting on the lives of the people there, but also from comparing theirs with my own.

Things I had taken for granted I now appreciate more. I have tried to put more time into the relationships that make my life and to see the value in the greatest resource of all – the people who make the places in which I live. I reflect more on how I am and how I propose to live. Rather than rushing towards the future I am trying to live to the full in the moment itself. The single most striking element I have learnt is that the pursuit of happiness should not lead you to the next thing that can be purchased, but to the next person with whom you can form a relationship. The exploration that awaits me is in the development of this and of myself. People make places, and the relationships and bonds you form there furnish the space.

(A full account of this trip is available in *Slí Eile/ Magis*, compiled by Padraig Swan. Dublin: Messenger Publishing Services, 2014, 76–84.)

Darragh Leonard is a PE teacher at Coláiste Iognáid SJ.

NOT JUST A SCHOLAR
A conversation with Hollie McDonnell
I always found that Crescent wasn't educating me simply to make a scholar of me; it was offering me education for my entire person, for my academic and other talents. Teaching is about making the learning experience better for others, so even after thirty years teaching, staff are still working to become better persons. The phrase 'Men and Women for Others' was one that always stuck with me. I was encouraged to improve my own skills and use my abilities and

my talents for everyone's benefit. That was a major part of school, no matter what your talent – whether in academics, or singing or choir, or sports, or creating something. It was not just a case of attending for six years and sitting your Leaving Cert and getting as many points as you can. Exams are important, but so is the experience you gain along the way.

Crescent community is like a family. I don't use that phrase lightly. It reinforced the reassuring message that I got from my parents, to be the best that I can be, to do what makes me happy, to be a leader rather than a follower. This made me very open to Jesuit education and to the *cura personalis* I found in Crescent. At another level, behind the scenes Crescent is like a well-oiled machine: everyone is part of it. There is a world of organisation behind the scenes, putting timetables and schedules together to make it work, but naturally as a student you see none of this! Now that I am back I realise how much cooperation it takes to achieve this.

The aim is to be the best you can be. To assist students, teachers give very willingly of their time. Everyone contributes. The school is very strong on developing an awareness of other people and their needs, and recognising the whole person. You are encouraged to be at your best for others, to do what you can. A fellow-student teacher who came from a different school background is very taken by the approach, but finds it takes some getting used to!

It is not hard to find something in your day that you are thankful for. To me, that is what the term 'finding God in all things' is about. When you have time to reflect, you take the small moments in the day, and you find things to be thankful for. In a community like this you are appreciated and you are made feel that you are worth something. When I was a student here, I was given an understanding of this from a teacher who made time to offer me a listening ear when I needed it. I deeply appreciated it. Later I was selected for a leading part in the musical, which was also a good moment, but it was surpassed by the memory of being heard by someone when I needed to be heard. That's what a Jesuit education is all about. That is a God moment! It might be only a tiny memory, which means something to me alone.

It's not a big public thing, but it shows the quality of what we are trying to do here. That memory inspires my own teaching. I always wanted to teach – in fact I know I have to teach! Yes, I love teaching my subjects, but more than that, I want to help students to have a love of learning. I feel very lucky to have identified what I really want to do, and I have the school to thank for that.

Hollie Mc Donnell is a trainee teacher and former pupil at Crescent College Comprehensive.

THE CHALLENGE OF COMPASSION
Peter McVerry SJ
In this short contribution I want to reflect on three issues:
What do we mean by a person of compassion?
How do we foster compassion in our students?
What are the consequences for ourselves in trying to do this?
What do we mean by compassion?
We often define compassion as a feeling of distress at the plight or suffering of another human being, which impels us to do something concrete immediately to alleviate that suffering.
We certainly want our students
- to have a compassion for those who are poor and marginalised in our societies;
- to commit themselves to analysing and challenging the structures that create and maintain poverty and marginalisation in our societies and in our world;
- to move beyond 'compassion for' the poor to a sense of 'solidarity with' the poor and a passion for justice.
How do we do this?
I think the 'See, Reflect and Act' framework is the way to go:
- We need to offer our students the opportunity of an intense experience of being with the poor, as St Ignatius and Pope Francis constantly remind us.
- We then have to offer them the opportunity to reflect on that experience. This requires us to invest time and energy in our own teachers so that they will have the commitment to solidarity

and that passion for justice that will enable them to support the students' reflection.

– We have to offer them the opportunity to act on that reflection.

What are the consequences for us?

The consequences for our own schools may be profound. Unless our *school structures* reflect this solidarity and passion for justice they will at best be ineffective or at worst a contradiction to what we claim we are trying to achieve. To develop people of compassion is not only a challenge to our students but also a profound challenge to ourselves.

Peter McVerry SJ is Director of the Arrupe Society, which provides housing and support for homeless youths.

TO KNOW, TO LOVE AND TO SERVE
Dermot Murray SJ

Over the years I have moved schools several times. The Provincial assigns you, and off you go. My time at Crescent College Comprehensive really opened my eyes, and I had been involved in education for many years at that stage. What was it about the place? The mix in the school made it a very dynamic place; we had people who were well off while others were struggling. We had boys and girls together, as it is a comprehensive school. I felt my time there gave me a richer understanding of the Characteristics. The phrase 'To know, to love and to serve' comes to mind when I talk about it.

What do the students take away from the experience? Do they grow into an understanding of what Jesuit education is about? I think they do. Looking back, I think they had a deep sense of being given something that they have to share, and in that, they understand what they owe.

Dermot Murray SJ is a retired headmaster of several Jesuit schools.

SERVING THE HUMAN COMMUNITY AND THE CHURCH

CLEARING THE AIR

There is a refreshing honesty about young people, and if we invite them to take a positive attitude to the Church, we do well, first, to be equally honest about its shortcomings. Only in this way can we clear the way for the presentation of this seventh characteristic. By 'Church' is meant here the Roman Catholic Church.

The Church is meant to embody *cura personalis* on a global scale. The divine intention is that it should radiate to everyone the *cura personalis* of God. But it has deservedly had a bad press over many years. Its darker side has been proclaimed in books such as ER Chamberlain's *The Bad Popes*.[74] The Crusades, the Inquisitions, the treatment of Galileo and innumerable other dark events have brought discredit to the movement established by Jesus to carry his message of love and mercy to a needy world. The Church has tortured the bodies of men and women in the name of God. It has tortured minds and hearts with its threats of eternal damnation. Most recently it has been found guilty of enabling and covering up clerical sexual abuse, together with cruelty to minors in some of its institutions. This has shocked the Catholic world and alienated many. The exclusion of women from full participation in decision-making and teaching remains a major shame for a male-dominated Church.[75]

The misuse of spiritual power is an endemic weakness in the Church. Today clericalism is one of the Church's greatest ills, according to Pope Francis, who has openly referred to it as 'the leprosy of the Church'.[76] Clericalism takes many forms: pride, power-seeking, self-importance, despising others, treating the laity as second-class citizens and disenfranchising women. The Church's tendency to exclusivism is evident in the ancient slogan 'outside the Church, no salvation'. Given that the sins of the Church are so glaring, it is not surprising that for many sincere people, the Church is a stumbling block rather than an aid to relationship with God. Its flaws are more obvious than its good characteristics. Diarmaid McCulloch, in his introduction to *The History of Christianity* (2009), takes a balanced approach:

My aim has been to seek out what I see as the good in the various forms of the Christian faith, while pointing clearly to what I think is foolish and dangerous within them. Religious belief can be very close to madness. It has brought human beings to acts of criminal folly as well as to the highest achievements of goodness, creativity and generosity. I tell the story of both extremes.[77]

The Church has its moments of humility and repentance. Vatican II makes its own the Reformation assertion that the Church is always in need of reform – *Ecclesia semper reformanda*. A tradition dating back to St Ambrose (d. 397) speaks of the Church as 'the chaste prostitute' – *casta meretrix*. Luigi Accattoli's *When A Pope Asks Forgiveness* reveals an unexpected dimension of John Paul II's pontificate.[78] By 1992 he had already asked forgiveness for the sins of the Church on more than 90 occasions, not however without protest from the Roman curia, who wanted to maintain the belief that the Church is a 'perfect society.'

AND YET ...

There is no disputing the specks and wrinkles (Ephesians 5:27) that have always disfigured the Church. And yet there is another side to the Christian community as it makes its pilgrim way through the centuries. The Good News has been spread across the world;

Gospel values have shaped European consciousness; the Christian Churches have 2.18 billion members. And just as Islam preserves the memory of Mohammed and presents him anew to successive generations, so the Christian Church testifies to Jesus. His memory is preserved through scripture and tradition, through the sacraments, and through the witness of countless Christians. The command to love has been expressed in innumerable works of charity.

While the Church is unequal to the task of carrying the treasure it has been given, it has retained its core conviction against impossible odds – the belief, founded on historical events 2,000 years ago, that God decided to pitch his tent among us in the person of an itinerant Jewish teacher named Jesus. For those who accept this claim, all is changed: human life is invested with new dignity and meaning, a new creation has begun (Galatians 6:15). To be human means already to share potentially in the divine. The task of the Church is to enable humans to encounter God in the person of Jesus. Through this meeting with the divine, a healing transformation takes place in the human heart, and life opens out in truth and goodness. When death comes, it is not the end, only a moment of in-between-ness, in which we are liberated from what is mortal and find ourselves caught into the radiant life of God.

HOLIER THAN THOU?

To dismiss the Church is to dismiss a large part of humankind. It may also be a way to dismiss the uncomfortable reality of humanity's flaws, from which none of us is immune. For us to accept the Church is to accept human brokenness and to acknowledge our own. We belong very naturally in this pilgrim group that keeps on losing its way. We think of the Church as old, but Christianity is one of the younger religions in comparison with Hinduism, Judaism and Buddhism. Perhaps only in our time is it arriving at early adulthood, having moved awkwardly though adolescence? Pope Francis says that the Church is our Mother – a flawed mother indeed, yet to be respected, loved and restored. In 1206 a young and carefree man, Francis of Assisi, heard the command: 'Francis, repair my house, which as you see is falling into ruin'. That challenge is addressed to Christians in every age, including our own. Pope Francis has proclaimed it in terms of evangelisation: the role of each and every member of the Church is to witness to the Good News. In the happy phrase attributed to St Francis, we are told, 'proclaim the Gospel. Use words if necessary!'

IGNATIUS AND THE CHURCH

Ignatius would say that Jesuits should be at the service of the Church, no matter how bad it may be. He had no illusions about it. He regarded the Church of his time, the sixteenth century, as being Christian only in name. Rome itself was a market where everything spiritual could be bought and sold. As a contemporary of Luther, Ignatius would have agreed about the iniquity of the Church. But where Luther decided that the only way forward was to protest openly against an institution that seemed beyond curing, Ignatius sensed that his God-given task was to serve the Church and to help to transform it from within. Hence his desire 'to help others' however he could, and especially by giving the Spiritual Exercises to carefully prepared people who would then influence others with Gospel values.

Ignatius suffered much at the hands of the Church. But this did not make him despair. His quasi-mystical approach to the Church led him and his early companions to offer themselves unconditionally to the Pope of the day so that he might send them to proclaim the Gospel wherever the need was greatest. He and his companions were known as 'reformed priests', by contrast to many of the clergy of their time. They lived under obedience and in poverty. They carried out a 'ministry of consolation', which contrasted with what was often a ministry of fear, and they served the sick in their homes or in what passed for hospitals.

Today, the phrase 'service of the Church' can be neuralgic to many good young people, whereas service to the human community is acceptable. Young people value freedom, and rightly so, because it is God's great gift to them. They have a deep desire to belong, however, and when they achieve this, they understand better who they are. They refuse to be dictated to, by clerics or anyone else, and they reject what they perceive as any unreasonable limiting of personal freedom, which can hide a de-valuing of the individual. Vatican II's phrase 'artisans of a new humanity' is likely to appeal more to young people than the notion of 'serving the Church'. They may argue from the Gospels that Jesus simply took people as he found them, helped them and then let them be, and that this is a healthier approach than herding them into an institution!

Instead of lamenting this wariness around the institutional Church, we would do better to look at the world through the eyes of the young, and to learn from them so that with them we *become* the Church that Jesus intended. Pope Francis offers us the choice between a 'self-referential Church' and one that is truly a servant of the world. The institutional Church has imploded over the last half-century, but with the support of the young we must struggle to reclaim the focus of its founder. God is *for the world*, Jesus is given *for the world*, and the Church is to be *for the world*. The Church is not an end in itself. Through study of scripture, through prayerful relationship with Jesus, and through discernment, the Christian community learns what sort of service is required truly to meet the deepest needs of humankind.

DISTURBING THE PEACE
The first Christians were charged with disturbing the peace, and in a deep sense it was true.[79] As an active community of disciples gathered round their risen Lord, their task was to awaken people everywhere to the fact that the Divine had irrupted into human history and that henceforth all relationships must be negotiated within the framework of divine loving and within the command to love one another.

The Church is commissioned to challenge whatever diminishes human dignity. One commentator, Walter Wink, argues that the task of the Church is to promote a domination-free society. This, he shows, is Jesus' work: this is what the Kingdom of God is about.[80] The Christian community is meant to protest against all forms of injustice, because everyone suffering discrimination is worthy of infinite human dignity, as a son or daughter of God. Fighting injustice is often disheartening and costly. To continue on the path, the Church at its best offers a much-needed community of support, the collaboration of like-minded and idealistic people who are energised by the power of the Spirit and the self-donating example of Jesus.

SUMMARY

Throughout history the Church has had many failings, and because it is human, these disfigurements continue today.

Ignatius' response to the call of Christ was to place himself at the service of the Catholic Church, despite all its faults.

Ignatius and his companions founded the Society of Jesus – and Jesuit schools – as part of the Church's mission to humanise the world and give glory to God.

The role of the Christian community is to sustain those who live out their faith, especially when they do so at great personal cost.

Like St Francis in the early thirteenth century, today we are to hear God say to us: 'Repair my house, which as you see is falling into ruin!'

The spiritual development of students of other faiths is an important value stemming from care for each individual.

SERVING THE HUMAN COMMUNITY AND THE CHURCH

LIVING EXPERIENCE

LIVING EXPERIENCE

JESUIT EDUCATION IN SERVICE OF THE CHURCH
Derek Cassidy SJ

Fundamental to the originating inspiration of the 'friends in the Lord' who founded the Jesuits in 1540 was the concept of service of the Church, to be expressed by availability to the Pope. They wanted to be sent *where the need was greatest*. As early as 1548, the friends put their learning at the service of a wider audience, opening a school at Messina in Sicily. Over the next 50 years the *Ratio studiorum* was developed, and was tried and tested down the generations by dedicated educators. From that move into 'forming' young men – and later, young women – the Jesuits served the Church in her core mission of education.

In the twenty-first century, Jesuit education continues to focus on the formation of young people who are gifted and graced by God, especially with the grace of compassion that notices those in the community who are most in need. Addressing these needs has typified the students of Jesuit institutes. It is summarised in the by now familiar phrase, 'men and women for others'.

This 'being for others' finds expression in a very rich array of 'faith in action' programmes. Some of these engagements have an enormous effect on the participants. In their own reflections they often speak of their experience as 'the best moment ever in my life'. Through these actions students take part in the life of the Church as they serve the needs of others, and commence upon the unfolding of their own faith life.

So, what does this service look like? Both you and I have seen many people sitting on the pavement with a paper cup held out in front of them. If you are like me, you will have avoided them while rushing past to nowhere in particular. Some students from Belvedere College found a way of addressing the need expressed by these members of our community: it has been christened the 'Soup Run'.

It takes place every Wednesday afternoon, even during school holidays. The students come in or remain on after class; they prepare soup and sandwiches, and head out to put into practice what they have heard in class, in prayer, in their own reflections and in the culture of the College: 'in so far as you did it for one of the least of these brothers and sisters of mine, you did it for me' (Matthew 25:40). They spend time with the people on the street: they sit with them, chat and listen. They offer not just soup and food, but respect and regard. In their conversation they offer eye-contact and recognition to the outcast.

The inspiration for this venture is a culture of awareness, handed down over the years by the student body, mainly under the aegis of St Vincent de Paul, and guided by the steady hand of Br Éamonn Davis SJ who, in turn, is walking firmly in the footsteps of previous generations of Jesuits who exercised a care for the needy. The service of the Church to the poor is very attractive to our students and staff, without whom it could not and would not continue. The soup run is always over-subscribed.

The St Vincent de Paul Society also gives students a golden opportunity to visit the isolated – those who are scared to go out, those who are unable to walk very far, those who are sad and lonely. The students sit with them, offering companionship, a listening ear and 'just someone to talk to'. One student recalls his shock on setting foot in the bed-sit of a pensioner who was too shaky on his legs to risk going out for groceries. 'It was something out of Dickens – packed, in my view, with rubbish. But this "rubbish" contained the precious possessions of his life's journey. Boy, did I need to readjust my categories!'

Some students choose Lourdes as their way of contributing: I think of this as service to the Wheelchair Church! The faith of the pilgrims is frequently what they notice, which gives them permission to sense, explore and touch their own faith: a graced moment, if ever there was one! Others volunteer to become eucharistic ministers; they serve in the College and in their local parish. It is planned to prepare lectors in the same way. This is a very useful service to their peer groups, to their families and to the staff.

The *Kairos* Retreat is run in many Jesuit schools. It is a 'peer ministry' and here in Belvedere it is made available to students in Poetry (fifth year), and is prepared, presented and delivered by Rhetoric (sixth year) students. Staff members also engage in the programme. It begins with a *Kairos* leaders' weekend away. The students select what 'talk' they will present; a long period of 10 to 12 weeks follows when each student meets the adult he has chosen and works up his presentation. It is in delivering that talk to the fifth year students that eyes and ears and hearts open – and Mystery occurs in our midst! That Mystery is frequently clothed in generosity of spirit, as the Gospel is received and refreshed and given a new set of clothes! 'I have always believed in God; but now I think we are much closer and I can see God present in others.'

Since the advent of Pope Francis, a freshness and openness characterises the mind-set of the Church, and his simplicity and integrity is attractive to young people in particular: he gives them hope in the goodness of humanity. As the face of the Church for multitudes around the world, Pope Francis is modelling behaviour and action that is attracting the next generation of men and women; there is about him a congruity that is inviting.

The students here are presented with an education that awakens them to the service of a needy community. Reflection on experience offers them options to continue this engagement. In time to come they will be the adult Church in Ireland and will, we hope, carry forward the mission of Christ – the proclamation of the Good News of God's compassion.

Derek Cassidy SJ is Rector of Belvedere College SJ.

PERCEPTIONS OF CHURCH
Jim Culliton SJ

For most young people a sense of belonging is critical in terms of their own view of themselves, and their growing awareness of who they are and how they fit into the world they inhabit. One of the corollaries of that sense of belonging is that generally they develop great trust in *the community* that comprises the institution. Witness the responses to invitations to participate, not only in 'in-house' activity, but to become involved in the lives of others outside the institution, especially the weak, poor and vulnerable. The concept that 'all gift is for giving away' is alive in our schools, in actions, if not necessarily in understanding. The natural generosity of the young, their desire to give and to make a difference is often overwhelming. They trust the invitations we offer – perhaps not least because the invitation is an expression of our trust in them. And so we experience across our schools all manner of creative outreach programmes in which young people have the confidence to expose themselves to many personal risks. In the process of the generous offering and the doing, they experience not only their capacity to give, to be generous with themselves and the courage to take risks; they also learn to be open to what those they serve – especially the poor – have to teach them about life and how to live it. When our students share this kind of work with one another, and particularly if they engage in reflection on it, they can experience a profound sense of community among themselves, as well as an understanding that a community is not a self-interested and inward looking thing.

You might think that the leap to faith and community – Church – should be a fairly simple task and a short journey. And yet, despite all our involvement, this is a great challenge to educators. I suggest two obstacles from my experience .

One is the current culture in which we live. Pretty well everything we encounter and touch in our day to day lives is understandable and verifiable. If we do not understand, we can work, study, question and explore, we can Google and get instant answers. We can switch stations if we are not stimulated by what is on; we get instant access to news, information, and even relationships, however virtual and risk-free they may be. Even in real relationships with friends, family and others, we can get instant feedback. The invitation to faith in and a relationship with the person of Jesus is of a different order and a huge risk, because it is a counter-cultural way of being in relationship with oneself, others and the world.

The second obstacle has to do with perception of Church. Many young people already have very strong experiences of community as essentially trustworthy and loving. In such community they have learned to tolerate and respect the flaws and weaknesses of being human. In general our young people are open to the possibility of faith in God, and in particular, relationship with Jesus Christ. They are confident in their relationships – up to a point – and confident in their capacity to make relationships. What allows them to take such risks, I believe, is because in all invitation, there is a strong sense of respect for the invitee, and in particular respect for the freedom of the invitee's response. I believe that this is why the young people in our schools respond so willingly and honestly to invitation.

But their perception of Church is that it is a community in which there is little freedom on entry, and less on remaining; little respect for dignity, little tolerance for difference, little freedom for choices. The perception is that the weak are not valued, that there is not a sense of fairness, that there is no place to be heard, that one's personal thoughts are irrelevant. Contrary to their experience in the various healthy groups they engage with, Church seems not to be an environment in which they will grow, be valued, and make an unique contribution. It comes across as a place where they will be told what to think, believe, and do, where if they make a mistake they may be excluded, where institution is primary and people and relationship are secondary. It seems a place where right relationships are defined, not discovered, where truth and justice are not valued.

These are the perceptions – and perhaps there is validity to them?

So the invitation we make to our students is a tough one. We believe that with all our flaws and imperfections – which are richly human – we are modelling Church, relationship and faith by our way of proceeding in the schools. We need to believe that the *Characteristics of Jesuit Education,* and the *Ratio Studiorum* which preceded them, have put us in touch with the vision Ignatius wanted to share with us, through his *Spiritual Exercises* and *Constitutions.* We can hope that we are engaged in carrying forward the work that Jesus began, in revealing us to ourselves, in revealing others to us, in revealing the world to us, and in revealing God to us. The vision of the trinitarian community is active and alive in our schools, and as such, we are *making* Church

- not an alternative version, but the real thing. We have received a great gift in the vision of Ignatius, who understood what it means to be human, to be a person in relationship with others, with the world and with God. We are passing on that vision daily in our vast array and styles of interactions, engagements and relationships with our students, and they with each other. At a very deep level, it is this which has excited me most about our educational enterprise. My experience of it constantly fills me with great hope for the future, not only of our world, but also of our Church.

Jim Culliton SJ has taught at Belvedere College SJ and Clongowes Wood College SJ for a total of 25 years.

ARMS OUTSTRETCHED TO THE WORLD
Eoghan Keogh

Jesuit education forms students 'for service of the Church'. I find that this is perhaps the most challenging of the characteristics to communicate to students. The most difficult aspect of this is that the Church they see is not one they fully desire to serve. So what is this characteristic trying to express? If 'service of the Church' were broadened out to mean the service of all its existing and *potential* members – which would be *all people* – this would exclude no one. The Church's role here on earth could then be seen as an expression of God's own love *for all*. Service of the Church could then mean the service of the whole people of God.

Is this a valid expansion of the characteristic? We need to start from an understanding of God's love for the world. We must look to its roots, to the limitless love shown in the life, death, person and practices of Jesus Christ. Jesuit education seeks to enable students to understand *this* vision of Church – a Church that promotes love and concern for all. Jesus showed this kind of love to the woman caught in adultery (John 8:1–11). He saw the person before the sin, and was more concerned with love and forgiveness than with the law. The same love is revealed in the parable of the Prodigal Son (Luke 15:11–32), where the father sees his wayward son and is more concerned with love than sin. Again, Jesus asks the paralysed man (John 5:1–8) if he wishes to be healed; he is moved by the man's disability. Always he sees the powerless before those who have power. He recognises the need to serve, include and love all, especially those who are outsiders.

The phrase 'Christ has no body now but yours' is attributed to St Teresa of Avila. This is what our Church is. It is Christ's body, reaching out to all, to members of the Church and also to people who feel outside it. This vision of Church is rooted firmly in the love shown in the Eucharist. Christ sat with the sinners and those who were religious outcasts. All are welcome at the table of God.

On leaving a Jesuit school students should have an understanding of this model of Church, one with its arms outstretched to the world. Its role is to welcome all, celebrate all, love and forgive all. In this Church students are encouraged not to be passive but to take ownership and leadership roles. When we gather at our Eucharist celebration, it's to celebrate the fact that we are loved unconditionally and that this love is never-ending. Love responds to love with love. The role of Jesuit education as a service to the Church in our world is simply to help form people to go out and serve with love. Jesuit education as an apostolate is an outreach of love. It moves beyond the pews of the church, into the everyday lives of young people, to journey with them and provide a space where they can grow. It helps students feel valued, understood, celebrated and cared for. Jesuit education seeks to be an expression of God's love.

Ignatius got involved in education as means of reaching more people with the message of love that he discovered in Christ. The hope for students in a Jesuit school is that they too will realise this love for themselves and, like Ignatius, will wish to share it in the Church, meaning the people both inside and out. The authenticity of their love and care will be contagious.

Jesuit students are encouraged to leave school not with a sense of embarrassment for what they have been given, but with a generosity of heart that is born of gratitude. Their sense of responsibility and of conscience is informed by love, not guilt. Their desire to respond to the needs of others emerges from a personal experience of being loved and valued. Jesuit education, in this context, is characterised by the practice of personal reflection, examination of one's own gifts and talents and the recognition of being loved and cared for. This is at the core of every student's development. Living in this awareness they notice the unconditional love given them by God through the people and experiences that fill the day. From this emerges their sense of being *invited* to respond to God's love just as Ignatius was. The choice is theirs.

Eoghan Keogh is chaplain at Belvedere College SJ.

THE CHARACTERISTICS AND MUSIC PERFORMANCE
Róisín Lavery

Music interweaves with many of the characteristics. For example, if we believe God is in everyone and all around us, then surely we serve God by serving others. Within the music department there are many opportunities to serve the school community through the choir and orchestra. I believe God puts us in places and situations for a reason, and that the members of the choir and the orchestra are there for a reason. Perhaps it is to learn about themselves, to be persons of conscience, to lead by example and teach others how to learn. Performing at a school Mass allows them to articulate their faith in a secular society. In my life I have always had music by my side. It is where I turn if the going gets tough.

When I ask the junior years to sing or play for a school Mass or concert I am met with terror! This feeling, I think, stems from inexperience and immaturity, but above all from peer pressure. By the time they reach fourth and fifth years they have largely overcome this fear. In a roundabout way I think the experience of singing or playing has itself done this for them. Here at Crescent we hold orchestra rehearsal at lunchtime. These teenagers would, of course, prefer to be out in the canteen with their friends. But they also enjoy the company of their orchestra peers; playing a piece through gives them a pleasure and a sense of achievement that is palpable in the music room.

If I am met with an initial reluctance to attend or perform I usually say, 'Well, if nobody performs then there is no performance.' When I coax them around to see that they are helping me and the school, they usually get engaged. Here is where the *magis* comes in! They are becoming men and women for others. A Mass without music, a Christmas assembly without a carol, a graduation without a final song ... ? On such occasions music would be greatly missed. It enhances the faith setting and enables people to feel something unique. A note or phrase may personally touch someone in the congregation.

Here at Crescent the hymn *Ad majorem Dei gloriam* has become a favourite. It helps students to identify with the school motto, and has a powerful effect on them. In primary school, I was influenced by a particular teacher – Sr Magdalen. I remember her telling me that I had a ministry in the Church because I was the organist. I believe music is a ministry, in which the members of the choir and orchestra help to bring God to their peers. This responsibility helps to develop them for life and for the service of others.

Musical performance promotes discipline, which permeates every part of adult life. It involves striving for excellence. The choir and orchestra have to turn up on time for rehearsal, stay together musically, stand and sit properly, watch the conductor. These are all traits of self-control. It also means getting involved, whatever your level or grade of musicianship. Individual care enables each student to fulfil his or her own potential.

I tell my music students: share your talents, show others what you can do, be proud, find your confidence! Look professional, even if you don't feel it. Don't undermine things by not performing properly: be aware of the perfect visual perception of sitting and standing correctly. Take the performance seriously and your audience will take you seriously. They won't laugh at you if you don't smile at them! As the song says, 'Walk Tall'. Perform brilliantly and those who say that being in the choir or the orchestra isn't cool will think you are very cool! Respect what you do, do it right and you will be respected. By being confident in music you become confident in yourself. Music is good for the soul and promotes healing and personal well-being.

Jesuit education promotes competence in men and women,

and music especially cultivates an appreciation of the creative arts. At Crescent students become more culturally aware through performances in Seachtain na Gaeilge. By developing our musical talents and being generous with our time and energy we are striving for excellence. However we couldn't perform without God's help.

Róisín Lavery is a teacher of music at Crescent College Comprehensive SJ.

OFFERING A *CATHOLIC* EDUCATION
A conversation with John O'Connor

We come through the Church to Christ. In Ireland, a challenge for anyone in religious education today is that the connection of people with the Church is greatly reduced. This reflects the general disillusionment with how the traditional Church developed here. It was experienced as being very clerical in structure. In some ways you could say that, in Irish society, Christianity was experienced vicariously. By that I mean that the Church did morality for us, so we did not have to work out our civic morality; it did the praying for us, and so we had an underdeveloped sense of personal prayer. People's religious education came nowhere near the depth of their general education; the Church 'did' theology for us. A disconnection emerged between our faith education and our adult life.

As a result, since the parents are the primary educators, it is very important that we have strong links with them so we can share the Jesuit approach with them. In my experience, this can be done by encouraging their participation in school activities. They send their sons to Gonzaga in the hope that they will achieve academic fulfilment, but they expect more in relation to their development. The liturgical calendar presents the opportunity to draw them into the faith side of things again.

I have two approaches with my older students. I offer a philosophy programme to the senior years, and I encourage the parents to read the textbook. I stress that civic morality and justice are concerns of the Catholic Church, to show that the course is not just about austerity or sexual morality. I also raise controversial questions about Catholic beliefs – such as 'was there a resurrection?' and ask them to discuss these subjects at home around the dinner table. In these ways I try to bring religious education out of the classroom and back into the home.

The concept of being 'a person for others' is attractive to students, and sometimes they latch on to it simply by fundraising for a worthy cause. While that is good, there is a lot more to it than that. The phrase is useful as it's a catch-phrase they will all remember. I see it as a real compass for them to direct their lives. The late Dr Garret Fitzgerald was greatly concerned to find a basis in the Ireland of today (and of the future) for a shared civic morality, which he felt was sadly lacking. A true Christian civic morality involves taking full responsibility for one's actions. It involves commitment to the common good, and demands the development of a shared sense of who we are as a people. It translates into a commitment to the poor, to the people struggling on the fringes of society.

The students here are blessed in having parents who care deeply about their education. They are likely to be able to access the careers of their choice and to be decision-makers in whatever profession they follow. Developing in them a sense of being 'persons for others' involves helping them to become enthusiastic for justice in society. I encourage them to see it as an everyday thing – doing what is right in the job that they normally do, or in the business that they run. When the time comes, their decisions will, I hope, influence people for the good. I want to plant the seeds of a lasting civic morality. I asked one young second year if he was a 'man for others'. He thought about it and answered that yes, he was. 'I can't always be thinking about myself'.

On one occasion we prayed in class for the father of a student who was undergoing surgery that day. Afterwards, we took a few minutes to think about what we had done, and we began to question what prayer actually was *for us*. Along with the request for healing, we realised that those praying might be invited to examine themselves and their possible contribution to the situation – to be the best they could be for a person, to offer their best support or professional assistance at that time. The boys felt that prayer was about accepting the reality of our lives, and opening up to embrace and bring excellence to what we do. It was interesting that they linked it to the other Jesuit trait of searching for excellence. The class that day understood something of the power of being there for others and the power of doing things well. I'll always remember it!

I have a deep sense that Ignatian spirituality is about the ordinary. It is about what *you* meet every day. It is about meeting Christ in those around you, but it always asks you to move forward and to be prepared to see things differently. It invites you to see the possibilities in front of you.

I start classes with five minutes of music. It allows the students to be still and to settle themselves. I present them with contrasts, a picture of Jesus on one wall, Che Guevara on the other. Both were concerned for the poor: we contrast their stories.

We have a history in education that was built on a tradition of excellence, but we have a new challenge to meet in the future, because we are now dealing with families who have little experience of Church or faith. We have a role to play in offering a Catholic education within that space.

John O'Connor is a teacher of religious education and philosophy at Gonzaga College SJ.

SEVENTH CHARACTERISTIC
INTENDING EXCELLENCE – THE *MAGIS*

WHAT IS THE *MAGIS*?

The word *magis* is a key term in current Ignatian usage, and brings us into the heart of Ignatian educational theory. *Magis* is Latin for 'more' or 'greater'. It underlies the motto *Ad Maiorem Dei Gloriam,* which all Jesuit pupils used to write on the top of their exercise books. The phrase means 'for the greater glory of God.' It was a favoured expression of St Ignatius: he was never content with the glory of God but sought God's *greater* glory. The term *magis* occurs some 170 times in the *Constitutions of the Society of Jesus*, which were written by Ignatius between 1540 and 1550, the decade after the Society was founded. It indicates the restless dynamism behind Ignatian spirituality. Jesuits regularly ask themselves, 'while this current work seems to be pleasing to God, would the service of some emerging need give God greater glory?' Which is the better of two good options?

THE WORLD OF CHIVALRY

The ideal of the *magis*, in the sense of doing ever greater deeds, was in Ignatius' blood from infancy. It was the defining characteristic of the world of chivalry into which he was born. A knight set great store by serving his lord, even to giving his life in his service. The sixteenth century was still a 'brave time' in European history. Ignatius' ancestors had lived by this chivalric code – while finding time to offend God in many ways! Ignatius was educated in courtly formation from 1506 to

1517, that is, from the time he was fifteen till he was twenty-six, and the *magis* framed his vision of the world and gave energy to life. He then went into knightly service. He read his books – *Amadis of Gaul* and other romances – and he studied the living models of chivalry around him.

Loyalty, honour, challenge and the desire to distinguish himself in service both of his Lord and his lady-love animated him. However futile the Pamplona episode of 1521 was, it vividly indicates what the *magis* is about, because there, against impossible odds, Ignatius decided that he must defend a miserable outpost against the might of the French army. Call it foolish heroism, because a leg injury brought his career as a knight to an abrupt end. Yet it was an admirable instance of greatness of soul, and it was later rewarded by his grateful lord.

THE *MAGIS* AT WORK IN IGNATIUS

God was by no means ignored in the chivalric attitude to life. *The Book of the Christian Knight* by John of Aliata was to hand, as was Erasmus' *Miles Christi* ('the soldier of Christ'). The young Ignatius would have been invested with arms in a *religious* ceremony – hence his later ritual disarming before the shrine of our Lady at Montserrat in 1522. There he left his sword at the altar and took the robes of a penitent, which represented his shift of allegiance from an earthly to a divine Lord. He later invites those engaging in his *Spiritual Exercises* to enter upon them 'with magnanimity and generosity' and to offer God their 'entire will and liberty' (*Spiritual Exercises*, n.5). For him mediocrity would not suffice in the service of God. Instead he invites his followers to radical generosity.

The process of *sublimation* drove his conversion. He slowly awoke to the reality of being personally called by Christ while he was convalescing in Loyola and reading *The Life of Christ* by Ludolph of Saxony. The movement is from the exercise of arms to the exercise of the spirit. The territory to be conquered and presented to God is now the world of human hearts. The limitless horizons of the Gospels open out. The goal of outstanding service remains, but now no longer service to the King of Spain, but to God to whom he refers often as 'the Divine Majesty'. Divine companionship replaces the distant relationship with a feudal lord, and Christ becomes central. He identifies with the Incarnate Son of God. He tries to be as much like Christ as possible: in poverty, humiliation, and in suffering. Most of all, the obedience of Christ becomes the model for his own, hence his constant desire to know and do what the Father wants of him. He experiences Jesus inviting him into intimate companionship, and so he has Jesus say, 'whoever wishes to *join me* in this enterprise must be willing to *labour with me*, that by *following me* in suffering, he may follow me in glory' (*Spiritual Exercises*, n.95). It is Jesus who leads the enterprise. Human companions – always important to Ignatius – now become friends in the Lord. This term was used in 1537 by Ignatius to designate the group, which later agreed to found the Society of Jesus, but early on it gained a wider connotation, and now embraces those who share the Ignatian vision.

Deeds would remain as the proof of a dedicated heart: 'Love ought to find its expression in deeds rather than in words' (*Spiritual Exercises* n.230). But they would not now be dramatic, self-absorbed exploits. Instead they emerge from prayerful pondering and an interior sense of what God wanted done in the here and now. Instead of conquering others, the task Ignatius now undertakes is summed up in the words, 'to help others' – a tiny but explosive phrase.[81] Only the honour and glory of God matter, but with the twist that *magis* gives: his constant search is for the *greater* honour and glory of God. This gave rise to the dynamic restlessness that characterises those who live out of Ignatian spirituality. For those who need stability, the unpredictability of Jesuit assignments can be unnerving: a man is doing good work in a school for years, and then is spirited away to minister to refugees on the far side of the world, leaving a void behind which others must struggle to fill. This recurring situation demands a deep trust in divine providence, a keystone in Ignatius' thinking. If God wants something done, God must provide the means.

This availability of the Jesuits for whatever God wanted done was the antithesis of monastic living. The monk thought in terms of stability, with an enclosed existence and an unvarying pattern of daily living according to an established Rule. By contrast, Jerónimo Nadal, one of the early commentators on Ignatius' Jesuit *Constitutions*, used to say 'The world is our home'.[82] Nadal intended to alert applicants to the Society that they would never put down permanent roots anywhere or, perhaps better, that they should indeed put down roots but be free to pull them up and replant as need and obedience required. In this quasi-nomadic style of existence, choice of place was decided by choice of ministry and, given the continuous change in human affairs, limitless freedom of heart and openness to travel were needed by Ignatius' followers.

For Ignatius, the central Rule was that his men should be always searching for what might *better* serve God. They were to keep God always before their eyes. They were sent on mission to a place and a work for a limited time, until the need identified there was met or handed over to others. They would then be sent off somewhere else. Hence the term 'shock troops' used to describe them, as they traversed the world and carried out impossibly diverse tasks. For many reasons the Jesuits lost this mobility over the centuries, but today it has re-emerged – perhaps most dramatically in the Jesuit Refugee Service, founded in 1980 by Pedro Arrupe, Superior General of the Society after Vatican II. Refugee crises can break out overnight, and Arrupe wanted his men to be available at short notice to leave fruitful, established apostolates and to enter into solidarity with refugees in whatever parts of the globe. Jesuits were to go where the need was *greater*, and where, perhaps, no one else was available to minister to the urgent requirements of the people of God. Thus in the criteria for Jesuit choice of ministries in Part VII of the *Constitutions*, the term *magis* recurs frequently.

A DYNAMIC IMAGE OF GOD
Behind the Ignatian ideal of the *magis* lies a dynamic concept of God.

Ignatius understood God to be active and engaged in this messy world, and to need collaborators. This image of God is portrayed in simple terms in a key moment of the *Spiritual Exercises* (nn.101-109) where the Trinity decide 'to bring about the redemption of the human race' and thus they engage Our Lady to set their plan in motion. The theme of God labouring and working is carried through to the end: 'God *works and labours* for me in all creatures upon the face of the earth' (n.236). Those in the Ignatian tradition must embrace this image of a creative and hard-working God, who responds to emerging challenges and chooses to need collaborators for the vast enterprise of 'the redemption of the human race'. Otherwise it seems like folly to prefer a life of 'helping others' to a comfortable and secure life. But Jesuits and their associates commit themselves to this availability. Perhaps Jesuits have the highest travel expenses of any Congregation, but one hopes that this is in the service of the *magis* alone, and not because they have itchy feet!

THE DISCERNING HEART

Here discernment comes in. If we are open to God and to the possibilities that life offers, we make our choices by referring to God. Discernment, whether individual or communal, means choosing the option that seems more pleasing to God, but it is not a shortcut through the labour of decision-making We must gather the facts; discuss options with whoever can help; try to be free of preferences for one option over another; spend time in prayer; mull over Gospel values, asking God to indicate what might best be done; notice the movements of the heart as we consider each option in turn; stay with the option that seems to respond to the steady drawing of God; and, finally, test our intended choice by seeking confirmation from whatever source is appropriate. We proceed then with the steady sense that we have chosen the wisest and most helpful course of action, even if it involves difficulty or hardship. The planned move should best take into account the needs of all concerned: it is this that will please the Lord. Those involved in Ignatian enterprises want to be like Jesus, who made no decisions without consulting his Father, and could therefore say 'I always do what pleases him' (John 8:29).

Perhaps enough has now been said to convey the strength of the word *magis* in Ignatian spirituality and Jesuit *praxis*. Now let us apply the concept to education.

EXCELLENCE IN SCHOOLS

Ignatius, we have said, was impatient with mediocrity. He grieved over people who used only a little of their ability, those who did enough to 'get by' but never excelled where they could. He saw people's gifts as precisely God-given for the service of the common good. With his deep sense of God's own greatness, he believed that God in turn invites us also to be great, and to commit the best of ourselves to meet the concerns of a needy world. A key word in his terminology is *todo*, meaning *all* or *everything*. The word recurs almost a thousand times in his writings. Half-hearted responses to divine invitations are unworthy of those who profess to follow a Christ who has given himself totally to us. *Magis*, then, means choosing the better of two *good* options. *Magis* stirs our generosity to make the better choice.

This quality is found in the dedicated work of teachers and administrators, who are constantly on the lookout for ways to serve their students better. It is also seen in students as they make their life-choices.

WHAT TO DO?

Let us imagine a middle-grade student who has completed her Jesuit schooling. She has enjoyed and benefited from it, and has internalised its values. Now she is stepping into a world of bewildering choices. But she wants to stay in tune with God as she moves along. So, what to do? She notices in her heart a desire to engage with the developing world before going to college. Her parents approve and offer the needed financial help. Then she wonders, *Will I be doing this just as a sightseer, as a spectator of misery?* Perhaps she notices a quiet desire to engage with a group that helps needy people to build homes for themselves. She gathers the data on this option. *What does this demand? Is it a really valuable project? Have I the health for it, and what skills do I have to offer? Will it damage my career prospects? Will it change my life forever, so that I lose touch with my friends? And what of my parents, who never got to College but would love to see me there?* She might find herself praying, *Lord, what would you like me to do?* She wants to make the wisest and best choice, and she watches out for the emergence of a quiet conviction that one or the other option expresses her best self and her deepest desire.

And so the process continues, until she makes her decision. The choice is hers alone: God waits respectfully. Then, mysteriously, a new joy comes to birth in her heart. In Ignatian terminology, this is called 'consolation' – that inner sense of being in harmony with God and with the divine project for our world. The *magis* involves a commitment to excellence. It says: *become your best self! Entrust your gifts to God and invite God to show you how best to use them. Respond to the expanding possibilities of his grace. None of us is on the planet just to do our own thing, or to fit in with what others expect of us; we are here to create something new.* Teachers can help pupils to identify their unique gifts and, with the help of the unforced rhythms of God's grace, to engage them for the service of the world. Those with the attitude of *magis* are open to change, development, evolution. They accord with Newman's comment that 'to live is to change, and to be perfect is to have changed often'.[83] Jesuit schools have a quality of openness to what is new, and they adapt readily to a changing world.

Finally, it can help to state what the Ignatian *magis* is not. It is not compulsion, driven-ness, the ill-advised personal striving that arises from perfectionism. It is not an obligation to follow someone else's dream ('this student must try harder!') nor an effort simply to do things for the sake of appearances. Rather, it is a prompting that emerges gently from within, through awareness of one's gifts, desires, and also one's limits. This prompting comes from the good Spirit and brings inner peace, a sense of consonance between myself and what I can become. God never asks the impossible, but invites me to that better goal which I *can* accomplish.

SUMMARY

Commitment to excellence is at the heart of Jesuit educational philosophy. This is the *magis*.

Ignatius' own life witnesses to what can happen in those who allow themselves to be led by the *magis*.

The Jesuit motto is *Ad maiorem Dei gloriam* – for God's greater glory. This means caring for God's disfigured world in the here and now.

Staff members witness to the *magis* in being generous with time and energy, and in searching out creative ways to help the students entrusted to them.

Students witness to the *magis* when they make the most of their unique talents and generously put them at the service of others, especially the less fortunate.

God does not ask the impossible, but invites us to some better goal, which we *can* accomplish.

INTENDING EXCELLENCE: THE MAGIS

LIVING EXPERIENCE

LIVING EXPERIENCE

CHARITY SUMS IT UP!
A conversation with Dermot Cowhey

You can define the core message of Christianity in all sorts of ways. For me, charity sums it up, and I think the *magis* – Striving for Excellence – has a great deal to do with charity and the message of 'giving'. How do you define *magis* for the students? We say to them: 'You have to be the best that you can be, not necessarily the best of all because that may not be possible, but the very best that you can be.' The message of Christ is Love, and this love is outward-looking so for me the concept of *magis* is the key to everything. To be the best that you can be is in the giving, and this connects with all of the other characteristics.

So, as a teacher, you have to have to be the best that you can be to empower students to reach their potential. In a Jesuit school you are called on to give more, and the giving can sometimes be hard: it makes demands of you. But it inspires you to give more – it's not just giving an extra class, not just being extra kind (when you don't feel like it) or extra patient; it is also about being available and welcoming to the child, even when the timing is not ideal for you. To achieve that degree of selflessness can be extremely difficult, but that is the challenge of everyday.

All of the characteristics come from the *magis*. It is out of this wanting the greater good for the person that *cura personalis* emerges. That is why Jesuit schools are so successful: they have always been person-centred. The teacher cares for the persons themselves, wishing that they may fulfil God's greatest desire for them. It's not about the 'subject' only, and it is certainly not about your ego.

Now, does everybody in all schools get that? No, but the major challenge is to get that to everyone, to invite everyone to share this vision, and to make that vision accessible to each staff member, not just to a core group.

Some people in the past were put off from the idea of 'seeking the greater good' because they thought it was only about seeking academic excellence, or doing school activities to a high professional level; or setting standards which might not be accessible to all. *Magis* is about 'giving' and 'not counting the cost' and this prayer attributed to St Ignatius opens with 'Lord, teach me to be generous'. It's about giving and not looking for thanks. It's about the child. It's about being content 'that I do your will'. So it should never be about 'me', it's always about other people and what God might want for them, and helping them to realise their undoubted, God-given potential.

When I retired from being Headmaster, people asked, 'Why not relax, and take the easy life?' I couldn't, because teaching in a Jesuit school is not about me. It's about other people. The Characteristics are apostolic, and they are about going out to other people and giving. You do this because you are a Christian, a Catholic. That is what Jesus in the Gospels did. We model our lives on him. Life was not about him; it was about humanity.

To catch on to this involves a journey of discovery, a gradual daily discovery. We struggle with it. It may be written down somewhere but you have to experience what life is about. This discovery is greatly helped by using the Ignatian paradigm of reflecting on experience and evaluating it in the light of your own appreciation of what is drawing out the best of you and what reflects your best desires in life. The *magis* is core to all of that.

How do you help others, especially new staff, to gain this insight? How do you help them to engage and to feel this energy in their work? You bear witness, and there are two elements to this. First, new colleagues can watch to see how it is done. To see people living it is worth many books. Second, they will hear and they will listen. A few years ago, in the Crescent, four staff members were asked simply to speak out of their own experience, and explain what their teaching meant to them. They were not all people known to have an especially religious outlook. To see them stand up and bear witness was a very powerful experience. People are not inclined to read books: but they will hear and they will listen. Often they see just one person whom they watch and admire. They wonder, 'how is it done?', or they invite you in by asking you to do something.

'Let your hearts go on fire with your charity'. That's it – the magis. *Induction* programmes give an important insight into what Jesuit education is about and the values we hold dear. We need to give new staff the opportunity to be inspired. Paradoxically, the reward actually comes with the giving. Perhaps you have helped some child walk a little bit taller, and you feel an uplift of grace.

The students get a chance to assimilate what is important when they go away on retreats. Over their six years in the school they are given various modules on Jesuit education and ethos and begin to understand 'Jesuit-speak'. The characteristics are spoken about, and give a good sense of the focus of the school. In the Captains' speeches on Graduation Day I have often been moved at how eloquently they can express what their experience was over the years here and what it has meant to them.

The parents are largely behind this, they are sending their children here because they identify that they want this for their children. They might get uneasy if you speak directly of Jesus Christ: but they are happy to see their child go on a 'sleep out' or a social outreach activity. They want what is good, what is best for their children – the *magis*. Many, at this stage, are past pupils themselves. They love coming back, and they express great satisfaction that the core ethos of the school has not changed.

As you would expect, staff responses vary. As a Church we have to acknowledge that we have done catastrophic things to people; yet this cannot take away from the good that the Church has done. There are a lot of people who continue the good work, but we are all struggling.

For my own part I take a characteristic every year and explore that. I was slow to take on the *magis,* because it is demanding. To be honest, I fail to live the *magis* most of the time but I keep trying!

Dermot Cowhey was previously headmaster of the Crescent Comprehensive College SJ and is currently teaching religious education, English and Kairos.

THE DYNAMIC OF THE *MAGIS*
Seamus Finegan

At the heart of Jesuit educational philosophy is the concept of striving for excellence. We see examples of this every day of the week. In terms of symbolism, we encourage the students to write AMDG on all their exercises, and on copybooks (*Ad Maiorem Dei Gloriam* – for the Greater Glory of God). To get the emphasis right, perhaps we should write it 'aMdg', because the emphasis is on doing what is for the *greater* good, what will be *most* pleasing to God. This is not about getting 100 per cent, nor is it just about your personal best. It's a focus on improving all the time. It also influences how you make choices and put effort into what is for the *greater* good.

I find that the staff commit to this ideal very readily. It translates into a willingness to be there, over and above what is expected on their timetable, at all times of the day. Belvedere is a place that never sleeps – and this creates an atmosphere where new people wish to excel; they want to make their mark. We encourage them to do that. They bring new ideas, new energy, and we foster this creativity, as this is how they will give of their best.

The staff has brought energy and innovation in the way that technology is used in the classroom. There is a great drive to improve the curricular subjects and to improve the students' educational experience. Bringing 'cool' technology to the fore really appeals to the students. It makes the classroom more interesting for everyone. Likewise, the co-curricular areas give plenty of opportunity for the staff to share their talents and enthusiasm. For example, we are all benefiting just now because some teachers are interested in exercise and nutrition, and are promoting personal fitness and healthy eating. There are gym sessions for staff and students, and we are signing up. There is even fruit in the staffroom! Enthusiasm generates energy – we would not have gone to the gym except for the encouragement and efforts of the new staff. Sadly a number of staff members have been suffering from ill health in recent times, so we have become more conscious of our own health. In order to look after the students we also have to look after ourselves better.

In what way do the students experience this striving for excellence, this reaching for greater things?

Around here, you hear the word 'invitation' used a lot. Even today at Mass, which was held to ask a blessing on those going to Lourdes, Fr Derek Cassidy reminded the students that they had accepted an *invitation* to go to Lourdes. We also let parents know of the many opportunities for new experiences offered in the College. The students are invited to take part; they choose to opt in. They are not compelled, as we need their commitment. We provide a richness of activities and this often involves difficult choices for students. They are asked to be generous with their time and talents, reflecting the opening of the prayer of St Ignatius, 'Lord, teach me to be generous, to give and not to count the cost'. This prayer encourages *excellence* in service to others.

A quotation from Newman struck me as very relevant to our desire to strive for excellence. He said, 'to live is to change, and to be perfect is to have changed often'.[84] To live out the *magis* we ask staff, students and parents to be open to change and growth. The challenge is there: if we find that we are not happy with the way things are, and if something can be done better – then go and *do* something about it! The *magis* – seeking excellence – provides a great dynamic within the school.

Seamus Finegan is the deputy headmaster of Belvedere College SJ.

ALL EXTRAORDINARY
A conversation with Declan O'Keeffe

The Jesuit system builds confidence, a good sense of self that should be related to concern for other people. At Morning Prayer if a student, maybe as young as 13 or 14, has achieved something (perhaps wins a sporting award) he is invited to address the whole school. I am so struck by the confidence of these young men. The school is asked to recognise their achievement, and often they will speak without notes: it's great to see them able to do this.

They also grow into a rooted concern for others, and this, at its best, is seen as a modest way of being. It is not arrogant; it is built on a belief in the worth of the person in front of them and it is carried over to their involvements after they leave school. This would be a good example of the quality I am thinking of: not long ago, when I was out in company, some past pupils came over to say hello. Among them was a lad who has gone on to play rugby for Ireland. They shook hands and he gave me his name, and the accountancy class year he was in, as a reminder. Of course I recognised him, but I admired the considerate way he did not expect everyone to know him: it was done very nicely.

In a boarding school, pupils are naturally strongly influenced by the school, but are also greatly influenced by one another. They learn a lot from one other; they stay in touch with one another. They are affected by Jesuit education, even if it is not delivered by Jesuits any more. But I think the staff understands what the school is about and they try to deliver that. On the macro level, the school tries to articulate what a Jesuit education is, and what the school is about. However, with the day job, the teaching, it's a subtext, and you try to integrate the characteristics with your subject matter on a daily basis, and demonstrate them through your teaching method.

Intending excellence - Be terrific! I like those phrases. I remember giving Morning Prayer to the boys earlier this year, and I was dissecting the prayer of St Ignatius. Taking the idea of 'to labour and to seek for no reward' (we should have difficulty with that, from a social justice perspective!) I said that this translates into being nice to others, doing small things like holding a door open for someone. Courtesy is much underrated, and it should not be either gender or age related - you should hold a door open for anyone, or stand when anyone enters a room. Politeness, respect, saying 'thank you' - all of these are small mannerly tributes to other people to show them that you see them, that you respect them. The boys are good about that. I ask them to settle for being extraordinary - that they are all extraordinary and we should try to be as extraordinary as possible.

I suppose I would want a new teacher to know that we believe that students are individuals, that they deserve the same respect as adults do - they are definitely not the enemy! Respecting them, you, as a teacher, have to be prepared to say that you don't know everything. A sense of humour really helps you to engage with them when, in the early days, you are nervous on the discipline front. I find now if you can be relaxed and allow things to develop, more emerges, and you have a better engagement with students.

Declan O'Keeffe is a teacher of history and head of communications at Clongowes Wood College SJ.

A COMMUNITY OF LEARNING

IS COMMUNITY MERELY AN OPTION?

'I chose my school for what I will get out of it – or at least my parents did!' This was an honest statement from a pupil who had just joined a Jesuit school. It is not surprising to hear such a remark, since instrumental values predominate in contemporary culture. Competition, capitalism, advancement by merit, the survival of the fittest – such values are accepted features of today's world, where the first question often asked is, *how will this affect me?*

There is a value in this question: it respects the process of individuation through which a child grows toward adulthood. But this dynamic is intended to occur within a context of mutuality. All I am and all I know is derived from others: how to speak and think and do, my attitudes and my values. We are ineradicably social, and our lives move into crisis if we become alienated from those around us. True education is in itself a communal event. But this requires a transformation of values, whereby students and staff commit themselves to the corporate project of learning. The more a school becomes a community, the richer in the students will the experience of learning be. In a tribute to the Jesuit Brother Michael Crowe of Colaiste Iognaid, Margaret Duggan writes:

> It was in the library that most of us met Brother Crowe… He was like the good shepherd in that he knew every book in the room… With his passing I began to grasp that the school is

more than an establishment – it is a community, and people like Brother Crowe make it special. His passing showed that there is a great bond between us that has real depth, however obscure it may seem sometimes. This sort of school spirit is a precious kind, which it is easy to be cynical about, but rewarding to believe in. It is a different spirit to that which is given an airing at a football match, or measured in academic success. It is a deeper feeling that will last long after we have left Colaiste Iognaid. The school will never be the same without Brother Crowe, but it is a better place for his having been there.[85]

WHAT *IS* COMMUNITY?

While a Jesuit school is to be a community of learning, it is not easy to define community. The term is often misused. It is more than a collection of persons gathered for a common enterprise. Community includes a common vision and shared work, shared joy and suffering. It involves bonding through mutual good will and affection. When the members of the group are in harmony, even on a transitory basis, community emerges. Easily disrupted by the myriad forms of selfishness, its maintenance requires ongoing commitment. Community endures a precarious existence, and is a miracle when it occurs. Its achievement demands deep respect for the styles and dreams of others, and a commitment to equality by which the unique contribution of each person is valued. A high point is reached when members come to love the others in their differences and idiosyncrasies. Community gives a sense of belonging, so that its members can say, *it is good to work here. I enjoy it, no matter how demanding the challenges are*. It is more than the sum of its parts: it is a new thing. It is strong enough to accommodate conflict, and in fact emerges the stronger when sincerely held differences are worked through.[86]

SCHOOL AS COMMUNITY

A school for which community is a central value provides a quality that other forms of learning cannot achieve. It is through our human relationships that we grow both intellectually and humanly. The Jesuit educational process respects both the uniqueness of the pupil and the movement toward community. The fostering of good relationships brings richness to school life, and the skills required to do this are central to the characteristic of individual care. A school that would let itself slip away from the value of community, through institutional abuse and bullying, would be hell. What we intend is the opposite, where everyone is *for* everyone else. This entails a deep willingness to serve the good of others, and creates an environment in which staff and students experience themselves as fully respected. The ongoing commitment to sustaining this ethos enables lasting friendships to develop.

A school is an inter-dependent system. What occurs in one area reverberates in others, to a greater or lesser degree. In a living and growing reality there are no permanent solutions: emerging challenges have to be creatively dealt with. Always the focus is the promotion of good relationships. In an atmosphere of teamwork and reciprocal acceptance everyone can become themselves, and know that they will be heard. Each encounter with others has potential for personal growth. Teaching and learning occur not only on the vertical but the horizontal dimensions. There emerges a mutual support that transcends differences of roles. Each child can say, *I am safe here, I belong, I can be myself.* Thus when they leave, students will have developed an inner confidence that liberates them to put their unique gifts at the service of others. As a Jesuit school community depends upon everyone's engagement, it also has the full range of policies and procedures to adhere to when people fail to live up to their obligations to others. Part of our mutual support of each other is to be prepared to acknowledge when things go wrong.

GOD'S PROJECT OF COMMUNITY

Community is not simply a human aspiration and construct. Christians believe that at its heart are the three divine Persons: they constitute the primordial community. The *social* nature of God is a central revelation in the New Testament. This signals God's intention that all persons, divine and human, should be in relationship. In creating us, the Trinity orientates us toward one another and towards community, which is both divine and human. We spoke above about our students becoming the artisans of a new humanity. This new humanity is being crafted into the final universal community, which is already gathering.[87] The drive to community is rooted in our very coming to be. We are formed through the intimate relationship between our parents, and we come ever more fully into being through family and wider relationships. Sexuality, so important to us, reveals immediately that we are not sufficient to ourselves; we are made for intimate relationship with another. We begin life in the community of family life, move to individuation and thus are enabled in our turn to foster community, which is God's central project.

HUMAN COMMUNITY TRANSFORMED

Jesus, the Man for all others, entered into the fragmented world of humankind to establish a new and enduring network of loving relationships. This is what terms such as *salvation* and *redemption* are trying to convey. The tortuous history of the Chosen People as related in the Hebrew and Christian scriptures conveys the drama of the sacred project, which is to irradiate all humankind with the divine. All that is good in human community is transposed into a higher dimension, and the three divine Persons act as the anchor for this new world order. The Gospel precepts provide the needed guidelines for creating and sustaining it, and the example of Jesus reveals it in practice. The work of God in our world is social and comprehensive: it takes account of all the elements to be integrated. The divine project will not fail. God thinks globally, and relates with individuals within that context. Our task is to carry forward the transcendent values of this new world order. The overall goal of the Jesuit educational enterprise finds its place here, in building this human-divine community. According to a Jewish story God asks each of us at the end of time, 'Did you enjoy my creation?' We suggest that more fundamentally we will be asked, 'Did you help to build my community?' Our students are to be carriers of the divine dream.

LOVE

Community and love are inseparable. Ignatius was reticent in speaking about love, and his followers are perhaps also slow to articulate its richness. Ignatius, a typical Basque, believed that love is found 'in deeds rather than in words' so while the word *love* may not be heard much in class and staff-room, the deeds that it expresses are found across the school spectrum. Love, like community, is an ambiguous term, easily misinterpreted. It runs from introverted self-love, through *eros* and philanthropy, all the way to divine love, which is often given its Greek name, *agape*.[88] The world is loved with *agape* (John 3:16), and our task is to share it without measure. It is to permeate all enterprises, including education. *Agape* goes beyond whim or feeling; it is a decision to love another, no matter what happens. It is enshrined in the marriage covenant – 'for better, for worse, for richer, for poorer, in sickness and in health'. Such a love does not fade if the person loved fails to respond; forgiveness is integral to it. Since God is irrevocably *for* us, we are to be totally *for* others, however variously that love is to find appropriate expression. The Ignatian desire, 'in all things to love and serve' (*en todo amar y servir*) urges generous hearts to donate their service to the human community. (*Spiritual Exercises* n.233)

Ignatius himself experienced the spectrum of love. He was ardent and passionate, and in his youth was known as a womaniser. But his heart also rose to courtly love. He fell for an unattainable lady of high rank and great beauty. For her he would have given his life. When he was convalescing after Pamplona in 1521, he daydreamed endlessly about her and the great deeds he would do in her honour. His capacity for the love of a woman was later translated into a tender and profound love for the Mother of God. Through his contemplation of the Gospels, his heart, he tells us, became ablaze with Jesus Christ. This expressed itself in an unrestricted commitment to the divine project for the human community. Loving identification with Christ meant seeing everyone as Christ sees them and loving them with his love. It was said of him in later life that he was all love and that no one went away from him sad.[89] Out of such love and vision the

Jesuit enterprise was born and flourished. Ignatius referred to his first companions as 'friends in the Lord', while Francis Xavier – one of those companions – used to speak of their companionship as the 'society of love'. Community, then, is foundational in the Jesuit vision.

At the close of the *Spiritual Exercises* (nn. 230 – 237) Ignatius reveals his heart and refers to God's unparalleled loving of us. 'The Lover gives and shares with the beloved what he possesses'. So, he says laconically, God gives us everything we need – creation, redemption and our particular gifts. Creation: the *resources of nature are given us so that we may grow to our full potential.* Redemption: *we are loved infinitely, as shown in the life, death and resurrection of Jesus.* Particular gifts: *we are uniquely graced and can make a distinctive contribution to the unfolding of human history.* The only fitting response to all this is gratitude, a dynamic virtue for Ignatius that begets the *magis* in us. Ignatius considered ingratitude to be the worst of sins, because it misses the fact that God is wholly good to us. As students grow to trust God as being limitlessly for them, they can invite God to accompany them on their life journeys. This constitutes community of the deepest kind. God can then work unobtrusively in their hearts so that with God they achieve great things.

'TO FEEL MYSELF BELOVED'

Love is our true destiny. We do not find the meaning of life by ourselves, alone, but with others. We labour to foster school community so that each student may be able to say *I am loved here.* 'Late Fragment' by Raymond Carver expresses what our students may rightly hope for from school life.

And did you get what
You wanted from this life, even so?
I did.
And what did you want?
To call myself beloved, to feel myself
Beloved on the earth.[90]

Jesuit schools are creative communities of life, work and worship. The inevitable mutual hurts that result from even the best of enterprises receive forgiveness through the healing presence of *agape*. We share a common vision of a world being made new, to which each has something unique to contribute. Community enables the growth of pupils both as human beings and as believers. All the stakeholders in a school form part of the educational community: pupils, staff, parents, board members, associates and all who, by their unobtrusive service, make the wheels of the institution turn smoothly. The role of religious belief in developing and sustaining such community is fundamental, because Christian faith endlessly reminds us of what God dreams for us, and how we may best achieve it.

SUMMARY

Community is God's intention for humankind. Its creation and maintenance are demanding. All the characteristics combine to strengthen the capacity for community in our students.

The more a school becomes a community, the richer will the experience of learning be.

Members of the educational community respect and care for one another as companions and friends, in the spirit of the gospel.

The love needed to hold the school community together is more than human. We call it *agape*, a distinctive love which is generously and ruggedly committed to the well-being of others, even at personal cost (see 1 Corinthians 13:4 – 8). Such is the love revealed in the life of Jesus.

A school community at its best localises the new world order established by Jesus Christ.

The Jesuit school community embraces pupils, teachers, administration, and also parents, board members, past pupils and those associated with the running of the school.

A COMMUNITY OF LEARNING

LIVING EXPERIENCE

LIVING EXPERIENCE

SERVING THE ENTIRE COMMUNITY
Louise Deane

I have contact with the new parents early on, and sometimes they are in a real state. They are delighted to be offered a place, but wonder should they go ahead – 'Is it the right decision for our son?' One mother came to me in tears, not knowing what to do. My answer was, 'When you see your boy graduating, you will be so proud of him.' I watch the boys mature. I see the love that the students and the past pupils have for the school. Even after many years they feel connected to the school and its traditions. Every child is different, but with the support and care they and their families get, most parents are delighted with how they settle in and develop. That mother came to me at graduation, six years later, and thanked me. Her second boy is now in the school.

It's hard to describe the support and care here. It is in the yard that you see the relationship that the teachers and the pupils have. Everyone is accepted. It's very equal. Everyone is allowed a voice. Everyone has a voice. They get the balance right. In the classroom the teacher might be in charge, but in the yard everyone relates on a different level.

Everyone in the school community matters, and there is a really positive atmosphere. The boys can relate to everyone. It's instilled into them to be grateful for the work that everyone does. You see the new students discovering that they are part of their new form; that they matter to their year; that they matter to their form tutor; that they are respected. That permeates the whole system. It gives them self-confidence and self-respect.

The pupils are offered a vast number of trips and experiences. They put in a lot of preparation for them and I can see how much they benefit. The trips might be short, but there are lasting gains – such as learning what life is like for other people, for those who are deprived. Each time they do the block pull for charity, at the presentation of the cheque they hear directly the real difference that their contribution is making to others in need. I see it with the lads. It does hit home, and it all adds up to the overall experience that we offer here. They begin to want good things and right things for humankind. The boys are so enthusiastic! So I, too, get a great sense of achievement. It might seem small, but I get a lot of feedback from their trips. With any group of young people, awkward incidents can and do happen. But you would be amazed how often people contact me to say they want to commend the group. 'They just know how to behave.' I think this comes from the sense of respect that they have been given.

They don't talk directly or openly about God or spirituality, but they readily join with the community of the school and sharing its values. They take pride in the school and in working with their friends on the projects they do, because they want 'to do the right thing for others'. Maybe, when they reflect later on about what they have done in the school, it hits home. Talking with their friends, you hear their pride in doing the right thing for others.

Recently we had a programme on the scholarship scheme shown on TV. Many did not know too much about it and were glad to discover more. They learnt that it offered opportunities to students who would not otherwise be able to come to us. But many liked the fact that this is normally done quietly, because honouring the person and his privacy is how the system works in Belvedere.

Given the large number of staff, you have the normal ups and downs of any workplace. There is always someone who will step into your day and make it worthwhile. It's only when you face a personal difficulty (for example, when a parent dies) that you really experience the depth of relationships. It really hits you then. The sort of conversations that you can have with people make you realise that you are relating on a different level, that God is working through this community.

Louise Deane is the administrator of school fees and manager of trips and exchanges at Belvedere College SJ.

WITH AN EYE TO THE FUTURE
Niall Leahy SJ

I arrived in Clane in September with all my earthly belongings, which happily included my golf clubs. 'If you're looking for me I'll be on the golf course!', I chirped as I set about making the most of the last week before school reopened. Time on the golf course provided a space for reflection. The question that surfaced in my mind was simply 'What's cookin' at Clongowes?' Not that I was worried about the quality of the food – it is delicious! I was more interested in the school's direction and trajectory. Before I arrived here I had heard many stories: 'the boys are a credit to the school – men for others', 'the results are excellent', 'it's like a family.' But for every impassioned supporter there seemed to be a detractor: 'rugby is the religion', 'private education is the preserve of the rich and entrenches economic inequality', 'Clongowes hasn't produced a Jesuit vocation in years.' It seemed like everybody had an opinion about the College. I wanted to form my own.

Two hundred years have passed since Fr Peter Kenney founded Clongowes in 1814. From my very first moments here I found the past to be very present here. Clongowes is full of memory, in the medieval architecture, the old portraits of boys on the walls and the long lists of headmasters and rectors. There's even a graveyard. Not that Clongowes is a museum! Many of the facilities are state of the art. There is a creative tension between old and new. Moving forward while preserving continuity with the past is very much a live issue now due to the diminishing Jesuit presence in the school. This development will represent the emphatic beginning of a new chapter in the school's history.

How will this go? My hunch is that the degree to which faith in the risen Lord is promoted and nurtured amongst the staff will have a large bearing on how the school fares. Why do I say this? There is a certain priority amongst the various characteristics of Jesuit education and for me faith is the one in which others can be grounded. Without having a relationship of some sort with God, virtues can easily become glittering vices. For example, excellence, when separated from faith, can become imbued with a sense of pragmatism which results in the person being primarily concerned with their own material wealth and comfort. By contrast, people of deep faith exhibit a sort of uncalculated foolishness, a reluctance to plot their own advancement, a readiness to give and not to count the cost.

To whom will we look as the main authors of this new chapter? The answer to that question depends on how far ahead we are looking. If we are talking about the next ten years, then it is the senior staff who will largely determine how the school fares during the imminent transition. Conversations with senior teaching and boarding staff alike reveal to me a reverence for the traditions which keep us connected in some way with the past. Life has also taught those with whom I spoke that we all ultimately rely on God. I find all of this very consoling. I have been incredibly impressed by their commitment to the boys' personal development, education and overall happiness. The pastoral instincts of the staff are finely honed and as a teacher-in-training I couldn't ask for better role models and mentors. I have no doubt that they will provide prophetic vision and leadership when called upon in the years ahead.

But if we stretch our horizons and think twenty five years down the line, then to whom will we look? One colleague mentioned in passing that I was the only young religious or priest-in-training that he has ever come across. Irish Jesuits are an endangered species! I would hope a good number of the current junior members of staff will still be around, and we can look to them. I've been bowled over by the quality of the characters who have taken up teaching and boarding posts more recently – hard-working, enthusiastic, personable, selfless. Remember, we're talking here about the generation that has supposedly walked away from God and the Catholic Church. I see openness to the spiritual dimension of life in them. This appreciation of spiritual things flies in the face of the current accepted narrative of secularisation. This openness can be nourished by offering access to the rich dimensions of Christian living and divine relationships.

At the moment, the Jesuits in Ireland are hopeful that a small number of younger Jesuits can keep the flame burning into the future. But it's wrong to say that the old guard is simply pinning their hopes on the younger guns. They do a lot more than hope; they invest generously in us younger men, with time, money, prayers and energy, so that we will be equipped to be effective ministers of the Gospel. Without this investment their hope would be idle. The demographic imbalance in the Jesuits is just a manifestation of a wider reality – the Irish Church as a whole is top-heavy with older people. The need to invest in the younger elements of the Church is greater than ever because the continuation of authentic Catholic education depends on younger generations waking up to the presence of God in their lives and in the world around them.

It is not for me to say how deep the faith of any staff member goes, nor my own. How many of us give quality time to prayer, or experience the peace that can be found in the chapel? How deeply is the love of Christ penetrating our hearts? I honestly don't know, but I'm not bothered because the only thing we need to be mindful of is that Christ can always penetrate our hearts more deeply. What's more, we have at hand an incredibly effective means to deepen our relationship with God – the Spiritual Exercises of St Ignatius. St Ignatius used to be very discerning about the people to whom he would give these Exercises. He preferred to give them to those who could bear most fruit. I am convinced that were he in Clongowes today, he would offer them to all staff, but especially to the younger members who carry the hopes of all for the future.

In short, I don't know what exactly is cooking – that will emerge in time. What I can say is that the ingredients are rich and plentiful.

Niall Leahy SJ is a Jesuit scholastic undertaking a Professional Masters of Education at NUI Maynooth and teaching at Clongowes Wood College SJ.

HOW I C LIFE IN A JESUIT SCHOOL
Anne Nevin

Community, collaboration, commitment, consciousness, concern, contemplation, challenge, culture, competition, care, conversation, choice – these are some of the words that come to my mind when asked how I see life in a Jesuit school. That I've omitted Church and Christianity from the list is not to be taken as ignoring them; rather I see all of these concepts as integral to my understanding and experience of Church and Christianity.

Creating men and women of 'competence, conscience and compassion' is the avowed aim of a Jesuit school.[91] This statement, with which I am long familiar, barely scratches the surface of the realities of a Jesuit school. What we are about is much broader. I work *within* a community, not *in* an institution. In fact I'm a member of a community, which sustains me, nurtures me and motivates me to achieve more. I am constantly challenged, be it through classroom contact, conversations with colleagues or by those rare moments for contemplation we can sometimes achieve in our working day.

This sense of community is evident throughout the school – from the moment you walk through the door in the morning you are enveloped in a cloak woven of care, concern and compassion. Some days the cloak is gossamer light, other days it resembles a warm blanket designed to banish the chills of the 'out there'. This sounds woolly (pun intended) but the small gestures of concern shown are some of the things that sustain me.

This concern for those around us extends well beyond the confines of the College. Students at all levels are offered, and take up, the challenges of going out into the wider community and using their varied skills for the benefit of others. It is one of the characteristics of the school that students see this engagement as a natural element of school life. The concern shown by our students to the residents of a community nursing unit nearby touched me personally when an elderly relative – not knowing from which school the students came – lauded their willingness to play Scrabble even when she was struggling to produce the simplest words. Such gentle generosity enriches us all.

The word 'collaboration', for a teacher of history and French, can have a certain pejorative ring to it. But when applied to our endeavours as educators it brings much of value to the enterprise. I am fortunate to have colleagues who appreciate that everyone benefits from collaborative teamwork. You will never be stuck for material for class use, you will never find yourself pondering too long on how to explain a particular concept to a student in difficulty. Someone will offer the perfect worksheet, the perfect accessible website, the perfectly reasoned argument to win a debate. That this should be apparent at all levels within the College is something to cherish. *Ar scáth a chéile a mhaireann na daoine* holds true for us all.

Life in a Jesuit school is so much more than an intellectual pursuit, but too frequently the wider world only comments on academic results. Within our small community our commitment to social justice and our efforts in this area are recognised. But why shouldn't we be crusaders for change? Men and women of conscience need *to act*. That is why it is so good to see staff and students collaborating on projects to share our gifts with others.

Such commitment is demanding, but when I commit myself I feel cherished, and it is this concern for me as an individual that keeps me engaged. Management has a significant role in ensuring this is in evidence at all levels – timetabling must see to it that nothing clashes with co-curricular activities in which staff are involved. Among the students, too, there is a level of commitment that is admirable, and without which our co-curricular life would not be as rich as it is. Hours are spent honing skills, preparing and delivering performances of outstanding quality. Here is 'excellence in all things' in action.

Each of the characteristics challenges me to move out of my comfort zone, to engage more fully with the chaos, to seek the consolation that is to be found in a job well done. I am called on to recognise the value of everyone, to care for those entrusted to me, to make choices, to commit my skills for the benefit of others, to cherish the opportunities offered; and, in turn, I am cared for. This is a Jesuit school – a community of which I want to remain a part.

Anne Nevin is a teacher of French at Gonzaga College SJ.

ONE COMMUNITY WITH THE SAME GOAL
Yvonne O'Brien

Belvedere is a very busy place, and naturally the focus is on how the students are developing and how they are reaching their full potential. In the past ten years we have sadly had a number of staff illnesses and deaths, and events in the school that have brought the school staff together. So in a way, we have broadened the term *cura personalis* to include care for the wider school community. We must include the staff since they are the ones nurturing the students and the parents.

We had an important day in December last year, when we got together as a staff to reflect on how we work, what we do and how best to support each other. We acknowledged how busy an environment we are in, and it allowed time for reflection to take stock of where we see Belvedere. There are some mechanisms to support staff. There is a Retreat in a working week and an induction programme for new staff. These may know the school only from the outside, and may have little sense yet of its spirit, neither do they know the staff mentors. The school has opportunities to thank the staff at end of year.

In the staff there is a great energy and a desire to excel! It's a little bit like osmosis; you are affected here by what goes on. For example, on a warm summer's day there are students around who are making soup and sandwiches for the homeless during the summer holidays. You could not fail to notice this! There are always students and staff onsite: they get locked in on occasion. Belvedere doesn't stop.

The school is known for its vibrant past pupils group. The door is always open. I've had past pupils who were working abroad come straight in to the school from the airport when they arrive back after many years. There is a great draw to come here. I suppose from the age of twelve to eighteen Belvedere has been their focal point; the school has introduced them to something of great value. Belvedere energises people – it is a school where it does not matter if you are interested in debating, golf, rugby, chess, the stage: every talent is applauded and respected. There is an openness to be involved and to take part.

For the new parents, we have introduced a forty minute video. It's images are mainly of the boys in action, the shows, the sports. It is hard to capture much of the academic dimension in pictures, but for many the video represents the experience of life in the school.

Parents want their child to achieve, so that he can go on to third level. The academic achievement is important because it opens that door. For many past pupils, opportunities in later life are opened up from school activities they participated in. But a priority for parents is that their child be happy and fulfilled. The measure of what people expect can be very different. Parents recognise what they want for their child; they know it in their hearts. It's most important to them that their child be happy and involved.

Because it is a caring community, the school asks more of people, and they respond. Just as for staff in any caring profession, work here is more than simply a job. Family becomes part of it. This is seen so clearly when someone suffers severe illness or loss: the wider school community is very supportive. People feel invited to live the life of the school. They become involved, give much of themselves and yet all say that they get back far more than they give.

It's extremely hard to quantify how deeply the ethos of the College permeates my role and my life! I can honestly say that whether it is the people I work with or those I engage with, there has always, for me, been a sense that I am part of a bigger picture and that we are all one community, working for the same goal. That sense of community is ever present in people's willingness to be involved in Belvedere and there is a huge pride in the College, its past, its present and its future. I know I am a better person for what I have learned from the students, staff, past pupils, and the Jesuits whom I been privileged to work with. For them, 'men for others' is not just a motto: it's a way of life.

Yvonne O'Brien is secretary to the headmaster of Belvedere College SJ.

YOU ARE WHAT YOU DO EVERY DAY
Declan O'Keeffe

I first came to work at Clongowes Wood College before any of the current pupils and even some of the staff were born. Mine was a late vocation to teaching, and Clongowes was different in those days. I was a 'live-in teacher' and we *never* returned to school before the start of September; classes ran from 9.15 to 16.00. We followed the same timetable each day, dined with the Jesuits in the castle, had an annual golf outing on Ascension Thursday and all three prefects were Jesuits. There were only 360 pupils: transition year had not yet arrived and the fourth years (still called Humanities) took 'O'-Level exams in the summer.

Twenty-seven years passed quickly enough, as I moved from being single to married to unmarried, and suddenly it was 2008 and I decided to take a year's career break, which eventually became four. I returned in September 2012 after four years of study. I came back to a different job, and wasn't a wet week in the place before I realised how much I had missed it. Not so much the college (although I had missed that too); it was more the job, the working with kids, the teaching. I have always been a teacher, and now I was lucky enough to be working as one and getting paid for it. Teaching is a brilliant job – if you *are* a teacher; if you're not, you shouldn't be doing it. Even if they are not attending a boarding school, children spend more time under the influence of their teachers than those of their parents, and that brings great responsibility and great opportunities.

I reckon I have taught more than 2,000 students. I meet past pupils from time to time by chance – such as at rugby matches – or by design, at class reunions and the Union Dinner. These are generally happy meetings but occasionally (rarely) a former student will confront me with an incident that occurred in class with which still rankles with him, and that he wants to clarify with me. Mercifully, owing to a fading memory, I never recall these events, and the conversation generally ends happily. The opposite also happens, and a past pupil tells me of something inspirational I said – some chance remark of mine in class that had a big effect on him and may even have influenced his life. Again, I never remember saying whatever it was.

Incidents such as these have often given me pause for thought – about the ways in which we teachers unknowingly affect our pupils, for good or ill. An unrehearsed remark can have a big effect. So what to do? We can't keep watching every single word that emerges, bidden or unbidden, for fear of *dis*couraging or in hopes of *en*couraging the boys we teach. That's like watching your feet as you run – you lose sight of the big picture and fall. All that we can do is to be honest in our thoughts and words as well as in our behaviour in the hope that our integrity will win the day.

Joe Schmidt, the Ireland rugby coach, tells his players: 'you are what you do every day'. *You are what you do every day*. If we strive to be good people, to do God's will every day and bear witness to our faith, our words and actions will reveal the goodness within, and good will follow. This doesn't just apply to pupil–teacher relationships, it informs our relationships with everyone: teachers, students, family, friends and those who do not fall into any of these groups. Be good to one another – and make a special effort when you don't feel like it. That's what Christianity is all about: loving your neighbour as you love yourself.

We are all here for a reason. Pope John XXIII said that his purpose in life was to discover God's plan for him and fulfil as much of it as he could. We may not all be that lucky. The American songwriter Jackson Browne wrote 'For A Dancer', in which he reflects on the nature of our relationships with one another and our purpose on this earth, which may be a mystery even to ourselves. He says: 'Somewhere between the time you arrive and the time you go / May lie a reason you were alive – that you'll never know'.

Every working day for nine months we, as teachers, engage with the pupils in our care and influence them. For us a class period may be a small slice of work, which, if we are having a bad day, may simply be something to endure. For us it may simply be another leaving certificate class; for them it is their *only* leaving certificate. For us it may be another bunch of noisy first years, who don't know how to sit still and be taught in an orderly manner; for them it is the start of a big, exciting, terrifying adventure that will mould them for life. Each class is a small, yet essential, step in that process.

I sometimes think that I could get through the course much quicker, if it wasn't for the pesky questions they keep asking, which slow things down. It's not as if I haven't explained it a thousand times already, for God's sake. Therein lies the danger. If we start to see the students as the enemy, then we have lost the battle. And they have lost too, because it isn't a battle; it's a co-operative enterprise where the synergy between the teacher's knowledge and skill, and the pupils' energy and talents transcends the humdrum of the classroom and amounts to a sum which is assuredly greater than the disparate parts.

And we do not know where that may lead.

Declan O'Keeffe is a teacher of history and head of communications at Clongowes Wood College SJ.

NINTH CHARACTERISTIC
ADAPTABLE AND OPEN TO GROWTH

SERVANT LEADERSHIP

If Jesuit education is successful, there emerges from it young people who are adaptable and open to growth. A recent Superior General of the Society of Jesus, Peter-Hans Kolvenbach, put it thus:

> We should recall that mediocrity has no place in Ignatius' world-view. He demands leaders who are in service to others in building the Kingdom of God in the market place of business and ideas, of service, of law and justice, of economics, theology and all areas of human life. He urges us to work for the greater glory of God because the world desperately needs men and women of competence, conscience and compassion, who generously give of themselves to others.[92]

Fr Kolvenbach spelt out what he meant. *Competence* embraces a broad spectrum of abilities – academic proficiency, including the capacity to reason reflectively, logically and critically; technological and vocational skills; an appreciation of the arts, sport and leisure activities; and effective communication skills. Persons of *conscience* discern what is right, good and true, and have the courage of their convictions; they take a stance to defend these values, have a passion for social justice and are influential servant-leaders in the community. Men and women of *compassion* respond to those in greatest need, walk in solidarity with them and empower them. They manifest a preferential love of the poor, revealed in concrete action. Clearly, this ninth characteristic of adaptability and openness to growth is revealed in those who aspire to be servant-leaders.

AN INTERLOCKING DYNAMISM

The last of the characteristics gathers up earlier themes, which taken together facilitate the emergence of servant leaders.

Firstly, human experience, when examined and reflected on, leads us along the road to truth and goodness, and enables us to find the beckoning God who is hidden and active in the depth of all life.

Secondly, care for the individual facilitates the growth of each student and fosters the awareness of personal uniqueness. This overflows into respect for the uniqueness of others, which plays a vital role in the development of community. A well-cultivated imagination develops openness to mystery, and enables students to move beyond all limited horizons to that which is unconditioned.

Thirdly, responsible freedom focuses gifts, skills and learning towards the service of the common good.

Fourthly, the friendship and companionship that develop from encountering Jesus Christ lead to a personal appropriation of his life-enhancing vision for the world.

Fifthly, a faith that does justice sees the world as God does, and labours with God for the growth of all-inclusive community.

Sixthly, the Church, despite its inadequacies, provides a living community, which enables ongoing encounters with God through the sacraments and the Word, and also the support needed to live out the Gospel. Religious literacy enables students to articulate 'the reason for the hope that you all have' (see 1 Peter 3:15), to enter sensitively into dialogue with those of other beliefs and none, and to move beyond differences in the common cause of serving humankind.

Seventhly, the ideal of becoming 'artisans of a new humanity' is a key aspect of the *magis*. It calls students to excellence in all its forms, but moves beyond self-development to take up the challenge of meeting the needs of the less fortunate. The human desire for greatness is realised in service (Mark 10:45).

Eighthly, a healthy school community provides a right appreciation of how the wider community of humankind can be developed.

ADAPTABILITY

And so we come to the ninth of the characteristics, adaptability and openness to growth. The Jesuit Order is characterised by an unusual capacity for adaptation. For Ignatius and his companions, as we have seen, the whole world, rather than some particular location, was their home, and they were to be ready to travel from place to place, anywhere in the world, as God might wish to send them, and for whatever tasks. It is true that the many colleges established in Ignatius' lifetime brought some stability to the image of Jesuit life. But availability for mission, wherever and whenever and however necessary, remained the underlying dynamic and has found a new energy in our day. In the Jesuit vision, adaptability is in function of service, and effective service is shaped by the process of wise choices, or 'discernment' in Ignatian-speak. But how can we consistently make wise choices? What is the Ignatian 'discerning love' (*discreta caritas*) so pivotal for wise adaptability?[93] We have touched on this topic before and now gather up its various strands, to indicate the parameters of Ignatian adaptability and openness to growth.

DISCERNMENT

'It began with an experience' – thus theologian Edward Schillebeeckx introduces his study of how the disciples of Jesus began to grapple with the world-shattering mystery of his resurrection.[94] Ignatian discernment was also born in the world of experience. While convalescing in Loyola, Ignatius, then thirty years old, divided his time between daydreaming about his lady-love and engrossing himself in the lives of Christ and the saints. Quite some time passed before he noticed a difference between the two experiences. The former left him dry and dissatisfied, while the latter gave him sustained energy and delight. This, he tells us, was his first lesson in noticing the diverse influences that play upon the human heart. There is a good influence, which leads us to what is helpful and good, and there are other influences that subtly draw us away from what is helpful and life-enhancing.

Ignatius developed a keen sensitivity to the moods of his heart, to the point that he would make no decision on his own, but always refer first to God 'as a wise and loving father'. He would then do whatever he believed God wanted done. On this point he was unshakeable, but was open to growth and change in regard to everything else. He believed, from inner experience, that God can play directly on the human heart and incline it in one direction or another, while leaving the person free. The art of discernment, then, is a becoming aware of that inner play and movement. Catching on to the drawing of God brings a sense of *consolation*, an awareness expressed in many ways, such as *this is me, I am being authentic. I am on the right path. I have energy for this task, even though it is difficult. Conversely, when I feel boredom, lack of enthusiasm and energy, I am, in Ignatian terms, being sucked into a downward spiral of desolation.* A school community that is trying to live out of the characteristics we have sketched is in basic consolation. No matter what challenges arise, there can be a strong conviction that God's approval and support is present. As one teacher put it, 'I feel the man above is backing us.'

TAKING DIRECTIONS FROM GOD

Jesuit education encourages in staff and students the growth of discerning hearts, that is, the capacity to reflect with God on daily experience and to learn its lessons. The Ignatian Examen or Review of Consciousness, mentioned already, enables God and ourselves to catch up. For busy people who have endless decisions to make it provides a welcome oasis in a crowded day. In this dialogue we first thank God for what has been good in our day; then review our decisions, ask to be shown what God wants us to do, and apologise for ways in which we may have spoiled God's plans. The interlude ends with asking God's help in what may be looming up ahead.[95]

The making of choices can be a complex affair, especially if communal or group decision-making is in question. A variety of hidden motivations can be operative, because the human heart, as the prophet Jeremiah remarked, is devious above all else; it is perverse. Who can understand it? (Jeremiah 17:9). Not only individual, but group bias may be operating. But at its core, Christian discernment means bringing God and Gospel values into our decision-making. No decision, however well-intentioned, has scientific certainty, but searching for God brings its own reward. We grow closer to God and become freer to adapt to changing circumstances.

To live in harmony with God means growth in interiority and the development of a discerning heart. The God of Ignatian spirituality is a God of surprises, hence the emphasis on adaptability and openness on our part. Life lived out openly with God is indeed a risk, but God does not play games with us. God needs us to play our part in building a better world, and shares with us the task of reading accurately 'the signs of the times' (Matthew 16:3). On our side, adaptability is not an excuse to do whatever we like. It is instead a sacred stance of openness to the living God, the God of relationships who engages us to be an escort of grace for every inhabitant on the planet.

OPENNESS TO GROWTH

What are the limits to human growth? Family, culture, peer pressures – these influence us, and we carry our innate physical, intellectual, volitional and affective strengths and limits. Without noticing how, we develop a self-image that is more or less authentic. But God is not limited by our situation or our image of ourselves, God sees us as good, very good (see Genesis 1:31). 'This Jack, joke, poor potsherd, / patch, matchwood, immortal diamond, / Is immortal diamond'.[96] We are formed in the image and likeness of a God who is infinite love and possibility. Therefore growth on the level of spirit has no limits, because God's loving of us is not to be equated with human loving: it is love of another kind. *Agape* is unconditional; it 'does not come to an end' (1 Corinthians 13:8). This love is in all students as a hidden treasure. We help them to appropriate it, live out of it, depend on it through thick and thin, and in short, to *become this love* of another kind. It is by sharing this love in manifold ways that we reach the fullness of our growth, and truly become gifts to a needy world.

Openness to growth is a priceless quality, which God can work with beyond our hopes and dreams.

A school living out of the characteristics is an embryonic realisation of the final community of love intended by God. It makes an ineradicable contribution to the final scheme of things. It is already part of the 'new heavens and new earth' promised by God in the final book of the New Testament (see Revelation 21:1 - 7).

SUMMARY

The world needs men and women of competence, conscience and compassion who will server humankind well.

Effective service is shaped by the process of wise choices, which we call Christian discernment. Staff and students develop the capacity to reflect on their experience and so find God. The Ignatian Examen or Review of Consciousness helps them always to keep God before their eyes.

Our task is to interpret accurately 'the signs of the times' (Matthew 16:3) and together to adapt to new challenges and opportunities.

The growth of students as persons has no inherent limits. Each in their own inimitable ways can come to match the mind and heart of Jesus, the Man for Others.

A school living out of the characteristics makes an ineradicable contribution to the final scheme of things. It is part of the 'new heavens and new earth' promised by God.

ADAPTABLE AND OPEN TO GROWTH

LIVING EXPERIENCE

LIVING EXPERIENCE

THE JOYS OF TEACHING
Jim Culliton SJ

I like to think that the purpose of Jesuit education is the great task of continuing the work that the Father has started in sending us his Son – allowing young people to go through a process where the truth about themselves, each other, the world and God is revealed to them.

Founded on the Gospels and the spirituality of Ignatius of Loyola, Jesuit education has evolved and been refined over time, keeping pace with the vast array of developments in our world, and yet its root purpose as hinted above remains the same. The *Ratio Studiorum* has recently been refined to the *Characteristics of Jesuit Education*. This latter document attempts to give flesh to that evolution, through reflection on local experience, and on the principles which underlie what we do. So, it is the *how* that changes, but not the foundation. In all Jesuit and Ignatian educational institutions there is a constant examination and reflection as to how things might be done better – *magis*! What gives underpinning, form, ethos, or charism to this constant reflection is the wisdom of the *Ratio/Characteristics*. It is in this way that the work of God continues in our Colleges.

I've had the privilege of working in Jesuit schools for the best part of 25 years, and I can't imagine any more exciting, rewarding and life-giving enterprise to have been involved in. That is not to say that there have not been times of pain, distress and disappointment. So, what has given me such joy and life, and hopefully allowed me to share that joy and life with others?

I love the fact that Jesuit education wants to educate the *whole person*, that it is not focused on narrow objectives; that the individual in community is at the centre of all the amazing array of engagement and activity in a Jesuit school – and the delightful tension that this brings. I love the environment of great energy and endeavour which characterise the young people as they engage in the process of questioning, seeking and discovery. Young people are naturally generous, and with the least encouragement they love to be invited to give of themselves. They also have a natural sense of justice and fairness, and constantly challenge the institutions to uphold these values.

It is important, I think, that all activity is considered *co-curricular*, as against the view that activity outside the classroom environment is an add-on. So I love the energy and enthusiasm of the adults in our schools, who are constantly seeking new means to draw out the myriad of talents and personalities that exist in the student group.

Among the key concepts and practices which mark out a school as a Jesuit school, one is the desire for excellence in what we do, each according to their own measure. We seek the *magis* for everyone, and that will differ according to gift, talent and desire. *Desire* is the key element, that desire to become the best you can be in what you do.

Another key insight is that *cura personalis* is in fact the responsibility of everyone. It should inform everything we do, and adults and students should be both its beneficiaries as well as its carriers. One of my great joys has been to witness moments when students are able to return that sense of *cura personalis*, and exercise it towards one another. Correctly, there is strong emphasis on eradicating bullying from our school environments, so it is wonderful to see not just an absence of bullying, but genuine care exercised by young people for one another, not just for their friends.

Those with specific pastoral roles accompany the students on their journey. This is a commitment on the part of the adult who stands with them in all that they do and experience; who respects their dignity; who carries them when necessary; who challenges them strongly at appropriate times; who defends them at other times; who celebrates their great moments, and empathises with them in darker ones; who over the years comes to know them deeply; who cares, and – if you like – loves them, in the most Christian of ways. I have always loved participating in the serious reflection that staff engage in about students . While sometimes done out of frustration and anger, almost always it is done out of care for the person. Likewise we encourage our students to reflect in differing ways, including prayer, on their experiences, more particularly on the variety of relationships they experience. And as staff we do this ourselves, so that we all learn from the experiences and challenge ourselves to relate better. Ultimately, I suppose, our desire is that we might all move beyond ourselves and our immediate relationships, to seek out bigger questions for ourselves, and therefore the possibility of a relationship with God.

One of the hallmarks of Jesuit education is that once 'reflection on experience' becomes a habit, there emerges the possibility of making good decisions. One of the pleasures I have got is through challenging students on their decision making – not that they should make decisions according to my lights, and therefore come to my conclusions, but much more a practice of ensuring that they consider everything necessary in the process. When they do that to the best of their ability, they are capable of making their best decision, whether I agree with them or not.

There is a high quality of relationship formed between staff and students. This occurs through the work that goes on, but also through the willingness of staff and students simply to engage in conversation – to waste time with one another, as it were. I have experienced joy through seeing so many different individuals grow in the confidence to reveal themselves and who they are becoming, and how they luxuriate in this fact themselves. Watch the young person who finds it hard to articulate, but has a gift for expressing herself through art; or another who might be shy, but takes the risk of taking part in a musical or play, and through the safety of costume, make-up and an asumed character, can reveal something of the wonder of who they are becoming. There is the boy who in the heat of battle on the sports field understands the meaning of team, and goes beyond self-concern to put his talent at its service. There is the quiet student who finds it hard to express the beauty of her talent and personality, but with the aid of a musical instrument – or her voice – can reduce you to tears of joy. There are pupils who in writing a reflective piece can reveal themselves in a way they might not yet have the confidence to speak, or who in a reflective exercise take the risk of expressing themselves to their greatest friends and harshest critics, and induce in their audience a sense of awe and a desire to grow in freedom to respond. Observe those who can forget themselves and show freedom of heart to respond to another's need; or who go beyond the immediacy of their world of relationships, and take the risk of believing in a God, not because they are told to, but because they want to. It is an awesome experience to witness young people reveal their depth and truth, and they too experience great joy when they become aware of themselves becoming more fully human – that is, becoming the persons God has created them to be.

Ignatian education is a very human activity, according as students and staff become more fully themselves. The harder exercise is moving to reflect on the role and relationship that God has in our lives and work, and the invitation to respond to this relationship. Thankfully we are unapologetic in declaring that we are committed Catholic schools in the Ignatian tradition, which has relationship with Jesus Christ as its ultimate goal. Born out of faith, we propose a relationship with God as both possible and as making the most sense out of everything that we do. We also encourage freedom in the students' response. What we do ask is that our conviction be considered at a profound level, and that then they make their own decision.

Jim Culliton SJ has taught at Belvedere College SJ and Clongowes Wood College SJ for a total of 25 years.

A MENU OF DEVELOPMENT
Grainne Delaney

The characteristics are very specific and the students leave here knowing about them. They might not be able to name them all, but they are very familiar with them. They are often drawn particularly to two or three which resonate more deeply with them.

Recently I have become interested in how images can be stronger than words and I have been searching to translate the concepts of the characteristics into images. We all know the power of a picture and how it can stay for a long time in our minds. I have found some images that the students really engage with. They are not religious icons, but they can be poignant and the students' response to them had led me further in my work of combining images and words together. If I can share the characteristics in a way that suits the learner best, then I think I am really succeeding.

In my work with different groups I have discovered different emphases; staff are different from students. I am glad that the induction programme for new staff sets out the values we promote and challenges teachers to be more Ignatian in their classroom. As staff progress in their own formation, I offer them a variety of opportunities to engage with the Jesuit ethos. I simply call it 'The Staff Ethos Menu' and people can choose, depending on their appetite.

People value gradual development and I would like to offer a sort of 'menu of development' that would allow for growth. I am also interested in how technology can support learning and formation, so that people can engage at their own pace, in their own time. I have prepared an on-line Course for Induction and Follow up. There is a great energy in the Jesuit Province around offering staff opportunities, which mean that our works and schools can continue to be Ignatian.

Grainne Delaney is the chaplain at Crescent College Comprehensive SJ.

WHAT ABOUT THE GOD PART?
Seamus Finegan

Jesuit schools overall have to be open to change. Our graduates should be identifiable as being open to growth in a changing world. How has this been reflected in the school, and what impact has it had down through the years?

Discovery and growth have enriched our interpretation of the *magis* over time. At first there was a tendency to understand it as academic excellence in an absolute sense, and so classes were streamed and an 'objective' excellence was sought. But this was found to be a self-defeating policy. With low expectations of themselves, great students lost out on their potential. So streaming and entrance exams were dropped, because they trapped people. This was a huge change, and many staff initially objected to it.

Then there emerged the insight that excellence was better served if *all* students were given the opportunity to excel. And rather than reducing overall performance, as some feared, this actually freed us to look at our students in a different way. Instead of pressure to measure up, there is an open invitation to excel. The culture of the school now seeks to serve the ambitions of all students. At the time, the change was controversial. But these changes are in keeping with the Jesuit philosophy of being open to new ways of doing things.

More recently, we have become more open to catering for special educational needs. Technology has freed us to look at new ways of teaching to meet learning styles. Some initiatives are driven from outside, from the Department of Education or international developments. But the teachers are open to worthwhile change from any quarter, and the need for change is incorporated into the 'striving for excellence' model. It's much deeper than medals or awards.

Teachers are encouraged to accept students for what they are, to deal with their unique talents. The Ignatian paradigm that encourages the study of context, experience, reflection, evaluation and action is taken in the context of the students' lives and their lived experience. We spend time getting to know the students as young men. Here the form tutors play a key role. Pastoral care in its many aspects is built into the school structures. Teachers and form tutors encourage evaluation and reflection on experience. This process is in the ether here! There are systems to promote it, such as the parent reply forms; we invite students to reflect, and we ask form tutors to evaluate and reflect on what is going on. Parents and students are asked to ponder examination results and reports – so that they become alert to underachievement, its causes, and its possible remedies.

The greater glory *of God*? You might ask, 'What about the God part?' We see that people are all at different stages on their journeys, but God is part of the equation here. We have an emphasis on faith that does justice; perhaps some might say that there is a huge emphasis on justice and less on faith. We may need to rebalance that for the future, as faith is the driver in the first place. But we have already created additional pastoral and chaplaincy roles, and a new director of faith and service activities has been appointed. While the first priority for staff is to teach well – the day job – there are also retreat opportunities for them. They are invited to see their role as supporting the spiritual development of the students. Form tutors are encouraged to go on the retreat programmes with their pupils.

Many of the systems we have in place are to encourage the students not just to be satisfied with making do; we want them to do more, to go the extra mile. While it is not all about awards, we have instituted an award ceremony throughout the years. It combines the academic and service dimensions within the school. We award medals and ties – the ties are very popular, and the boys wear them with pride! It's our way of saying 'Well done'.

Seamus Finegan is the deputy headmaster at Belvedere College SJ.

REACHING FULL MATURITY
Eoin Guidera

I work in a school that supports children experiencing high-functioning autism, behavioural problems and psychiatric issues, which can affect their day-to-day relationships. The children often find it hard to go beyond their own needs and anxieties. Moving from family relationships to playing and cooperating in the learning environment make great demands on some of the children. Guiding the children to be 'apostolic instruments' in this learning environment poses significant challenges for everyone in this school community.

Working with a group of twelve- and thirteen-year-olds preparing for confirmation I was charged with the responsibility of instructing them in the basic truths of the faith. Generally the class is interested, lively and engaged. The typical issues and questions arise for the children: *why does God let suffering happen? What is the point of making our confirmation? What do we really believe?*

The class, of course, learnt about the gifts of the Holy Spirit, drew and coloured the tree with the fruits of love, peace, faithfulness, patience, kindness, self-control and gentleness. But I got the impression that this lovely tree that they were drawing lacked roots. There was something missing that could make the confirmation preparation more of a reality for the children and myself. I had been chatting with a friend about this, and he happened to have used a large foam cube to illustrate the New Commandment. Each face had a different facet of the New Commandment printed on it: Love Everyone, Be the First to Love, Share the Other's Joy and Hurt, We Love One Another, Be the First to Love, Love Your Enemy. I explained the cube as a 'Good Deeds' cube.

With very little introduction, we started to roll the cube. The children were eager to tell their stories each day. Here's what John had to say one morning:

> I was with a group of my friends and this not very nice guy came over and wanted a go of my scooter. He kind of pushed everyone around a bit. My friends said "Say 'No!' for a go on your scooter." After my friends left he was still hanging around. I remembered we rolled "Love your Enemy" that day in school so I just gave him a go. My friends saw him coming down the road on the scooter and they were really confused. But I had decided to be the mature one.

Anne told a story about giving a present to her brother for his birthday:

> My older brother didn't get me anything for my birthday and I was really disappointed. A few weeks later it was his birthday. I had got a present of some money for my birthday. In school that day we had rolled the cube and it said "Be the first to love" so I went out and used some of my birthday money to buy him a present.

After hearing a few experiences like this I decided actually to read what was in the resource pack that came with the cube. I noticed that there was a prayer and some ideas for each face of the cube. The children took to this, too, and we added it to our daily routine (they're the ones reminding me now). I began to see that this simple foam cube was the seed that we needed to grow in openness to the gifts of the Spirit. We started using the cube as a new way of talking about our hurt, disappointment, anger and anxieties.

We explored what we might do with the cube. It was the children who came up with the idea of rolling the cube each day as one of their commitments for confirmation. I decided to push the boat out a bit and asked the class if they would also commit to introducing one of the younger classes to the cube.

During the confirmation ceremony, after the class had introduced the cube to their parents and families, a present was made of it to the communion class. So the confirmation class got a chance to experience their own Pentecost as they passed on the faith to the younger children.

I'll finish with one of my favourite stories told by Áine:

Every morning I play my Nintendo DS on the school bus with another boy. We play Super Street Fighter 4 3D edition. I kept spam attacking him so he could never win. He was getting really annoyed at me. But that day in class we rolled the cube and it said "Love your enemy" so on the way home I decided not to use my spam attack fighting strategy so he could get a chance to win.

The psychologist Igor Caruso is quoted as saying: 'Relationships should be open to a transcendent "You", after overcoming the final obstacle that stands in the way of reaching full maturity; one's own self'.[97] This is, for me, the essence of being an 'apostolic instrument'.

This is how John described the same idea using the cube:

We pass it on to others. We can spread it on to other kids and try and achieve the motto for the day. We come in with great stories. And the toughest one is "Love your Enemy". If we accomplish this we get mature.

Eoin Guidera is a class teacher at St Declan's Special NS, Dublin.

RELATIONSHIPS AND PRACTICES
Claire Lohan

Fundamental to the ethos of any Jesuit school is the emphasis that is placed on mutual respect and positive relationships between staff and students. These help towards holistic, personal, spiritual and intellectual growth. Within this climate of mutual respect and trust, students are more likely to recognise their own unique strengths and reach their true potential both within and outside the classroom context. Positive relationships will flourish where the students feel that they are cared for individually by every level of the school structure, from the board of management to the auxiliary staff.

A key factor in building on mutual trust and respect is the ability to empower the students by giving them extra responsibility. This added autonomy instils confidence and self-belief in them and helps them to identify their own abilities and embrace the uniqueness of others.

Students should feel free to express themselves honestly and freely, but always within the understanding of mutual respect, and in compliance with the code of behaviour. In fostering a positive climate of trust and openness, those responsible for the college need to be compassionate in their interactions with the students and in the decisions they make. Students and staff will be more equipped to deal with the changing needs and demands of the world today when they are cradled in this caring and compassionate environment.

Positive relationships are promoted by compassion, respect and listening; by taking time to stop and talk outside the classroom, and praising the students wherever it is warranted and celebrating their success; by encouraging all students to reach for the highest grade that they can get, and by discouraging mediocrity. It may be the more challenging student who needs guidance. On the other hand, the quiet student can go unnoticed and may be the one who needs attention and care to be brought to a new level of understanding of their own beauty and uniqueness.

School policies and practices encourage students to self-reflect and self-evaluate. Schools need to adapt to rapid changes in the world of education, for instance, in their policies for admission, bullying, literacy and numeracy. Policy formation encourages us to look at the way we do things and forces us to respond to new needs. Practices are informed by policies; language, tone and directives are all very important in ensuring that the right message is conveyed and that the policy supports the ethos of the school.

With fewer Jesuit teachers, lay staff need an understanding of Ignatian spirituality. There are structures at Coláiste Iognáid to ensure that this takes place. An ethos coordinator promotes the Ignatian vision in the school and arranges visits and outings, which enrich our understanding of Ignatius. 'The footsteps of Ignatius' is an annual pilgrimage to Spain for staff and parents. New staff members are invited to an induction weekend, which informs them of the values and attitudes that characterise Jesuit education. The Ignatian identity group invites parents and staff to build on the foundations of the ethos as a direct response to the depletion of Jesuit numbers.

Kairos retreats, which are peer led, help adolescents find their own personal relationship with God. Annual Retreats, school Masses, religion classes and regular assemblies are opportunities to deepen student and staff understanding of Ignatian spirituality. Iconography helps by depicting the life and work of Ignatius Loyola.

Social outreach is an opportunity to work with and help communities who are less fortunate. This increases student social awareness and competence, and gives practical shape to Ignatius' dream of helping others wherever possible.

Claire Lohan is a teacher of business and maths at Coláiste Iognáid SJ.

THE ONE WHO GIVES GLADLY
Pauric Madden

After almost forty years I can still say I love teaching; I love my subject; and it is a privilege and a pleasure to work with boys and young men, and to be part of their journey of learning and discovery. I have no doubt that I have been significantly influenced, both personally and professionally, by the fact that most of my teaching life has been spent in a Jesuit school. 'Each one should give what he has decided in his own mind, not grudgingly or because he is made to, for God loves a cheerful giver.' (2 Corinthians 9:7)

Teaching is more than imparting knowledge; it is more than measuring a product. Teaching demands that I get to know my students, that I am curious about them, that I am interested in them as people, that I want the best for them even if they themselves cannot see that. If I don't aspire to a generosity of spirit in the way I treat my students, by respecting them and encouraging them to respect each other, I have little chance of fostering generosity or a love of English in them. However, it is always important for me to start where they are at, to learn what they know and like, rather than to impose my expectations immediately.

I am lucky in my subject. Being a teacher of English allows me to engage in a real and concrete way with the lives of young people: with the mystery of who we are and why we are here. Teaching English also allows me to challenge attitudes, opinions and behaviour that are counter-productive for living life fully. If I am not striving for better ways to teach my subject, if I am not seeking more creative or effective methodologies, how can I demand that my students strive to improve, to aim higher or produce better quality work? I make a point of reading several novels per year that are aimed at young people; it helps me understand better what's going on in their world.

At a very basic level, I encourage my students to be generous. Boys will frequently and understandably look for the short cut, the minimum response. I tease them into writing more, to giving me more than they think I want. A first year class group needs to be encouraged to find the goodness in each other, to respect the opinions of one another. Later they need to be challenged to accept difference, to be tolerant and supportive of those who are on a different path from themselves.

In first year one of my pet projects is working on basic punctuation, especially the apostrophe. I form a 'Campaign to Protect the Apostrophe' and encourage my students to find instances in everyday life where the apostrophe is misused. Learning occurs as much in the world as in the classroom, and students are encouraged to engage critically with that world from an early age.

Teaching for me is about more than imparting writing skills or encouraging a love of literature. English offers many opportunities for addressing life-skills, for developing a generosity of spirit, for fostering an openness to the new and an appreciation of the blessings we possess.

The challenge for the older student is to find the goodness in himself, to come to know himself through personal writing and reading, to take a risk in revealing who he really is and to come to a sense of being happy in his own skin. We read the classics for wisdom and for an insight into the human condition through exposure to universal themes. When we read great literature, hopefully we are inspired to emulation. We dream, we hope to be the best that we can be. We hope our students are inspired by the literature they encounter in the junior and leaving certificate syllabi.

In transition year there are opportunities for doing things differently. I try to wake them up. If I can encourage them to open their eyes and ears to the world around them, they are already on the road to becoming storytellers. If I can encourage them to open their hearts and minds they begin to empathise with and also challenge the world around them. I find that, for the most part, I teach by stealth. Through contemporary literature, music, film and graphic fiction I push them to engage with the new, the untried, with less well-known texts, artists and directors. I try and link what I teach to the many opportunities students have in our school for social justice activities, for taking themselves out of their comfort zones.

Students often live in the immediate, seeking instant solutions to difficulties, instant gratification for their desires. Modern media create a focus on quick communication; messaging and texting rarely deals with anything beyond the now, the next short time. They offer rather quick-fix solutions to complex problems. When the social world dominates the lives of our students, particularly into the early hours of the morning in chat rooms and online gaming sites – the world of school, study and homework can become unreal and less relevant.

It is the teacher's role to challenge that situation, to stimulate an interest in the longer view, to model more authentic and genuine relationships and life experiences through the subject he or she teaches. By stressing the value of more, by urging the value of generosity, by modelling the value of pursuing excellence, we can turn our students on to life as it really is and away from the notion of instant success and gratification. The teacher's role is to plant the seed, to encourage the student to focus on the journey, to reflect on and engage with the world rather than to race through it collecting trophy experiences on the way.

Pauric Madden is a teacher of English at Belvedere College SJ.

BE THE BEST THAT YOU CAN BE
Éamonn McGuinness

It was the poor Franciscans who had to educate me, but now I am enjoying a second education, a Jesuit education by osmosis, because my children were and are going through the Jes. So what have I learnt so far?

I have learnt that *magis* is a term closely associated with Jesuits. In Ignatian terms it refers to the philosophy of doing more, for Christ, and therefore for others. It is an expression of both aspiration and inspiration. Ignatius would encourage his companions to ask: *what have I done for Christ? What am I doing for Christ? And last but not least, what MORE can I do for him?*

Now this is pretty heavy stuff for young students, especially for the significant percentage who have no real interest in faith formation. However I have seen that in the schools *magis* is not – at least initially – communicated thus. I have seen parents at school meetings get upset when they hear it described as 'striving for excellence', as they are afraid that their children are being pushed too much and compared too much with other students. But in the Jes I have heard it clarified many times: it is not about comparing children, rather it is about *being the best that each person can be* – to use one's unique gifts and talents fully. I have also seen it linked with that other Jesuit motto – 'men and women for others'. *Magis* is all about being the best that you can be in order best to help others. *Magis* is not about being the best you can be in order to accumulate vast wealth or fame for yourself, but rather to help others. AMDG – for the greater glory of God and others, and not of oneself.

The *magis*, and being the best that one can be, are definitely in the lexicon of the Jes. As a parent I find this very important. The world is a cynical place and a school should be a place of optimism. Young people should start their lives with hope. I have also learned that Saint Ignatius favoured deeds over words. Therefore in the school we can assume that the best Ignatian way to teach pupils about *magis* is to lead by example. Pope Paul VI, in his 1975 encyclical *On Evangelization in the Modern World*, observed that 'modern man listens more willingly to witnesses than to teachers, and if he does listen to teachers, it is because they are witnesses'.[98] I have seen first-hand so many teachers in the Jes who give much more of themselves to the pupils than is asked of them. They do this in and outside the classroom. They deliver for others and so give effective witness to the *magis*. It is about these teachers who lead by example that our gang talk with love at our dinner table. And I love the Jes teachers for this positive example.

I have also heard Jesuits explaining that *magis* means to 'go deeper'. Quality over quantity: less done *really well* rather than more done poorly. To be the best that you can be, you have to go deeper into yourself. The students have to reflect – they need time out to think. The latter is hard in today's noisy world – but it is an important part of young life and it is vital for the *magis*. Last week I heard an exchange between two students. One had recently switched from the Jes to a 'grind school' to get the points he needed for medicine. His friend, still in the Jes, asked him if students had any time in the grind school to think about life. The grind school pupil laughed at this ridiculous prospect and said they had no such luxury. The asking student was horrified!

As a parent enjoying Jesuit education from the sidelines I, of course, want 'more' of this in a Jesuit school! As an employer in business I see many young people not taking enough time to think before they act. Ignatius required that Jesuits would take a short time out at least once or twice a day – the daily Examen. Like the *magis*, the Examen is at the very core of the Jesuit way of proceeding. We all need to go deeper to do more, to be the best that we can be. I would love to see this simple but powerful practice nurtured more.

Our young students are entering a fabulous but tough world. We need to challenge them to be ready to do more for the world they are entering. Here are three great Jesuit examples that I find inspiring – clarion calls to do more, to go deeper.

Pope Francis recently delivered a call to *magis* action:

Authentic faith always implies a profound desire to change the world. Here are the questions we should ask ourselves: do we have great visions and dash? Are we daring? Does our dream fly high? Does zeal devour us? Or are we mediocre and content with our laboratory apostolic programs?[99]

Fr Peter McVerry concluded a paper on 'The Compassionate Person' as follows:

We must offer our students opportunities to experience the world of the poor, to reflect in a systematic way on that experience, and to take action to make the world a better place. This may, and sometimes should, lead to a reflection on the nature and role of the educational centre itself.[100]

Ignatius wrote to King Philip II of Spain as follows: 'all the well-being of Christianity and of the whole world depends on the proper education of youth'.[101] In our schools we are doing nothing less.

So, back to my own Jesuit education. The biggest lesson that I have learnt as a parent is that while the school plays its part, the real responsibility for magis education lies at home. School and home indeed collaborate, but I have learned that the buck stops here! I am very grateful for this Jesuit education I am receiving.

Éamonn McGuinness is a parent at Coláiste Iognáid SJ.

SOURCES

There is an immense literature relating to Ignatian spirituality and Jesuit education, and some 800 websites. The primary source for this book is *The Characteristics of Jesuit Education*, published in 1987 as the charter for Jesuit schools. Composed by an international commission which met over four years and consulted worldwide, it in turn is based on the insights of St Ignatius Loyola, on the educational tradition that has developed since the first Jesuit school was founded in Sicily, and on best contemporary practice. Here are given a few pointers towards recent and accessible literature.

An Ignatian Spirituality Reader, edited by George W Traub. Chicago: Loyola Press, 2008.

A Jesuit Education Reader, edited by George W Traub. Chicago: Loyola Press, 2008.

Jesuit Secondary Education Association, *Foundations*, new edn (Washington, DC: JSEA, 2005), available at http://www.jsea.org/sites/default/files/resources/attachments/Foundations.pdf.

Brian Grogan, *Alone and on Foot: Ignatius of Loyola*. Dublin: Veritas, 2008. (An abridgement of *Solo y a Pie* by Tellechea Idigoras.)

Diccionario de Espiritualidad Ignaciana. Bilbao: Ediciones Mensajero, 2007.

WEBSITES:
www.ignatianspirituality.com
onlineministries.creighton.edu/CollaborativeMinistry/daily.html

ENDNOTES

1   Jesuit Secondary Education Association, 'Instrument for Self-Evaluation of Jesuit High Schools', in *Foundations*, new edn (Washington, DC: JSEA, 2005), 18, at http://www.jsea.org/sites/default/files/resources/attachments/Foundations.pdf.

2   Diego Ledesma, 'De ratione et ordine studiorum Collegii Romani', in *Monumenta paedagogica Societatis Iesu*, edited by Ladisalus Lukács, Monumenta Historica Societatis Iesu, volume 107 (Rome: Institutum Historicum Societatis Iesu, 1974), 528–9; translated by John W. Padberg, 'Development of the *Ratio studiorum*', in *The Jesuit* Ratio Studiorum: *400th Anniversary Perspectives*, edited by Vincent J Duminuco (New York: Fordham UP, 2000), 97.

3   See Adolfo Nicolás, 'Depth, Universality, and Learned Ministry: Challenges to Jesuit Higher Education Today', 23 April 2010, available at http://www.sjweb.info/documents/ansj/100423_Mexico%20City_Higher%20Education%20Today_ENG.pdf, accessed 6 October 2014.

4   Juan de Polanco to Antonio Araoz, 1 December 1551, in Ignatius of Loyola, *Letters and Instructions*, translated by Martin E. Palmer, John W. Padberg and John L McCarthy (St Louis: Institute of Jesuit Sources, 2006), 363.

5   Bruce Bradley, 'The Characteristics of Jesuit Education', available at http://archive-ie.com/page/878262/2012-12-08/http://colaisteiognaid.ie/home/jes_identity/jesuit-education/24-jesuit-education.html, accessed 6 October 2014.

6   John WO'Malley, *The First Jesuits* (Cambridge, Ma: Harvard UP, 1993), 220.

7   See http://www.sjweb.info/education/stats.cfm, accessed 23 July 2014.

8   The commitment of the Jesuit Order to collaboration is most recently expressed in 'Collaboration at the Heart of Mission', *Decrees and Documents of the 35th General Congregation of the Society of Jesus* (Oxford: Way Books, 2008), decree 6.

9   Irenaeus, *Adversus Haereses*, 4.34.5–7.

10   Plato, *Apology*, 38a, quoting Socrates

11   Ignatius of Loyola presumes that the person making his Spiritual Exercises has the capacity to reflect on inner experiences, otherwise there can be no serious dialogue with the one giving them. At the end of the *Exercises* he repeats three times, 'I will reflect' (nn.235–237).

12   'East Coker', in TS Eliot, *The Complete Poems and Plays* (London: Faber, 1969), 186.

13   The original phrase 'men for others' was the title of Pedro Arrupe's address to the Tenth International Congress of Jesuit Alumni of Europe, 31 July 1973, available at http://onlineministries.creighton.edu/CollaborativeMinistry/men-for-others.html, accessed 23 July 2014.

14   For an expansion of this idea, see *From Teilhard to Omega: Co-creating an Unfinished Universe*, edited by Ilia Delio (New York: Orbis, 2014).

15   John Paul II, *Faith and Reason* (London: CTS, 1998). The Pope asserts that philosophy is one of the noblest of human tasks, and that truth and freedom go hand in hand or together they perish in misery. 'Faith and reason are like two wings on which the human spirit rises to the contemplation of truth' (3).

16   Pope Francis, *The Light of Faith* (Rome: Libreria Editrice Vaticana, 2013), nn.1–6

17   I shall be using the English translation by Louis Puhl (Chicago: Loyola Press, 2010).

18   See *The Constitutions of the Society of Jesus and Their Complementary Norms* (St Louis: Institute of Jesuit Sources, 1996), X.1[812]

19   Ignatius, 'Reminiscences (Autobiography)', n.27.

20   Ignatius was a theologian in his own right, though not an academic one. His orientation was towards service of God, and his mysticism has been termed a mysticism of *service* rather than of union. See Hugo Rahner, *Ignatius the Theologian* (London: Chapman, 1968).

21   For an introduction to the life of Ignatius, see Brian Grogan, *Alone and on Foot: Ignatius of Loyola* (Dublin: Veritas, 2008). An abridgement of *Solo y a Pie* by Tellechea Idigoras.

22   James Joyce, *A Portrait of the Artist as a Young Man* (New York: Viking, 1968), 253.

23 Bernard JF Lonergan, *Insight: A Study of Human Understanding* (London: Longmans, 1957). Lonergan sees the pure desire to know as fundamental to being human. It is central to cognitional development, dynamic and unrestricted, and is an instance of the desire for God that all creatures have. 'The immanent source of transcendence in man is our detached, disinterested, unrestricted desire to know' (636).

24 See www.aacu.org/leap/what_is_liberal_education.cfm, accessed 23 July 2014.

25 See Jean Vanier, *Made for Happiness: Discovering the Meaning of Life with Aristotle* (London: DLT, 2001).

26 For a brief outline of Ignatian humanism, see *An Ignatian Spirituality Reader*, edited by George W Traub (Chicago: Loyola Press, 2008), 10–15. For more, read Ronald Modras, *Ignatian Humanism: A Dynamic Spirituality for the 21st Century* (Chicago: Loyola Press, 2004).

27 See John Kenneth Galbraith, *The Age of Uncertainty* (Boston: Houghton Mifflin, 1977).

28 This fundamental Ignatian idea appears often in Ignatius' writings; see, for example, Ignatius to Antonio Brandão, 1 June 1551, in *Ignatius of Loyola: Letters and Instructions*, edited by Martin E Palmer, John W Padberg and John L McCarthy (St Louis: Institute of Jesuit Sources, 2006), 342.

29 See CS Lewis, *The Weight of Glory* (New York: HarperCollins, 2001), 46.

30 Thomas Merton, *Conjectures of a Guilty Bystander* (New York: Image, 1968), 158

31 Gerard Manley Hopkins, 'The Leaden Echo and the Golden Echo', in *Poems of Gerard Manley Hopkins*, edited by WH Gardner and NH Mackenzie (London: Oxford University Press, 1967), 92.

32 See Pierre Teilhard de Chardin, *The Divine Milieu*, translated by Siôn Cowell (Eastbourne: Sussex Academic Press, 2004).

33 GK Chesterton, *St Francis of Assisi* (New York: Doubleday, 2001), 88.

34 See Karl Rahner, *Theological Investigations*, volume 10, translated by Edward Quinn (London: DLT, 1981), 149.

35 For this radical option of Ignatius, see Grogan, *Alone and on Foot*, part four.

36 For more on the role of the Christian at meetings, see Phyllis Brady and Brian Grogan, *Meetings Matter: Spirituality and Skills for Meetings* (Dublin: Veritas, 2009).

37 Patrick Kavanagh, 'The Great Hunger', in *Collected Poems* (London: Allen Lane 2004), 70.

38 Nuala O'Faolain, *Are You Somebody? The Accidental Memoir of a Dublin Woman* (New York: Henry Holt and Company, 1996).

39 Andrew Solomon, *Far From the Tree: Parents, Children and the Search for Identity* (New York: Scribner, 2012).

40 Merton continues: 'At the centre of our being is a point of nothingness which is untouched by sin and by illusion, a point of pure truth which belongs entirely to God. It is never at our disposal, and from it God arranges our lives. It is inaccessible to the fantasies of our own mind or the brutalities of our own will. This is the pure glory of God in us. It is so to speak his name written in us, as our poverty, our dependence, our reality as daughters and sons of God. It is like a pure diamond, blazing with the invisible light of heaven. It is in everybody…' Thomas Merton, *Conjectures of a Guilty Bystander*, 155.

41 Aristotle, *De anima*, 3.8.

42 Ignatius, 'Reminiscences (Autobiography)', in *Personal Writings*, translated by Joseph A Munitiz and Philip Endean (London: Penguin, 2004), n.27.

43 Ignatius, 'Reminiscences (Autobiography)', n.87.

44 John Henry Newman, *An Essay in Aid of a Grammar of Assent* (Notre Dame: Notre Dame Press, 1979), 89

45 For the ideas in this paragraph I am indebted to Michael Paul Gallagher, *Dive Deeper: The Human Poetry of Faith* (London, DLT, 2001), 9–11; also his *Faith Maps* (London: DLT, 2010), 14–16.

46 Seamus Heaney, 'The Rain Stick', in *The Spirit Level* (New York: Farrar, Straus and Giroux, 1997), 3.

47 Marianne Williamson, *A Return to Love: Reflections on the Principles of a Course in Miracles* (London: HareperCollins, 1996), 191.

48 *Characteristics of Jesuit Education* (London and Dublin: British and Irish Provinces SJ, 1987),

18

49   Mary Oliver, 'The Summer Day', in *New and Selected Poems* (Boston: Beacon Press, 1993), 94.

50   See http://www.europeansocialsurvey.org/, accessed 23 July 2014.

51   See Pope Francis, *The Joy of the Gospel* (Dublin: Veritas, 2013), nn. 35–43, 93–127.

52   Plato, *Phaedo*, 114d.

53   See CS Lewis, *Mere Christianity* (New York: HarperCollins, 2009 [1952]), book 4.

54   Teilhard de Chardin, *The Phenomenon of Man*, translated by Bernard Wall (London: Collins, 1970).

55   Henry Wadsworth Longfellow, 'My Lost Youth', in *Poems and Other Writings*, edited by JD McClatchy (New York: Library of America, 2000), 337.

56   See Lonergan, *Insight*, 687–730.

57   Khalil Gibran, 'On Children', in *The Prophet* (London: Vintage, 2013), 19–20.

58   Adolfo Nicolás, homily at Crescent College, 11 September 2009, available at http://www.youtube.com/watch?v=TPb54xU6ZNY (accesed 8 October 2014).

59   Greg Boyle, *Tattoos on the Heart – The Power of Boundless Compassion* (New York: Free Press, 2010), 87.

60   *Decrees and Documents of the 35th General Congregation of the Society of Jesus*, decree 2, n.2.

61   Dignitatis humanae, n.2.

62   Hopkins, 'Thee, God, I come from, to thee go', in *Poems of Gerard Manley Hopkins*, 194.

63   See Friedrich von Hugel, *The Mystical Element of Religion* (New York: Crossroad, 1999).

64   See Pope Francis, *Joy of the Gospel*.

65   Patrick Kavanagh, 'If Ever You Go to Dublin Town', in *Collected Poems*, 192.

66   'Eleven Facts about Global Poverty', https://www.dosomething.org/facts/11-facts-about-global-poverty, accessed 23 July 2014.

67   *Gaudium et spes*, n.30, available at http://www.vatican.va/archive/hist_councils/ii_vatican_council/documents/vat-ii_const_19651207_gaudium-et-spes_en.html, accessed 23 July 2014.

68   *Gaudium et spes*, n.1.

69   See 'Justice in the World', http://www.shc.edu/theolibrary/resources/synodjw.htm, accessed 23 July 2014.

70   Society of Jesus, *Thirty-First and Thirty-Second General Congregations* (St Louis: Institute of Jesuit Sources, 1977), 411–438.

71   See Jennifer Preston, 'Malala Yousafzai, Girl Shot by Taliban, Makes Appeal at U.N.', *New York Times* (13 July 2013), available at http://thelede.blogs.nytimes.com/2013/07/12/video-of-malala-yousafzai-at-u-n-calling-on-world-leaders-to-provide-education-to-every-child/?_php=true&_type=blogs&_r=0

72   From https://www.dosomething.org/facts/11-facts-about-global-poverty.

73   Hopkins 'Felix Randal', *Poems of Gerard Manley Hopkins*, 87.

74   ER Chamberlain, *The Bad Popes* (New York: Barnes and Noble, 1994 [1969]). In the same vein, see Peter de Rosa, *Vicars of Christ: The Dark Side of the Papacy* (London: Corgi, 1988), and Gary Willis, *Papal Sin* (New York: Doubleday, 2000).

75   See Mary T Malone, *The Elephant in the Church: A Woman's Tract for Our Times* (Dublin: Columba, 2014).

76   'Francesco a Scalfari: così cambierò la Chiesa', *La Reppublica* (1 October 2013), available at http://www.repubblica.it/cultura/2013/10/01/news/papa_francesco_a_scalfari_cos_cambier_la_chiesa-67630792/, accessed 23 July 2014.

77   Diarmaid MacCulloch, *Christianity: The First Three Thousand Years* (London: Penguin, 2009), 13.

78   Luigi Accattoli, *When A Pope Asks Forgiveness* (New York: Alba, 1998). Among the topics are the Crusades; collusion with dictatorships; schisms and religious wars; and the Church's treatment of women, Jews, the Reformers, Muslims and scientists.

79   Eamonn Bredin, *Disturbing the Peace: The Way of Disciples* (Dublin: Columba Press, 1993).

80   Walter Wink, *Engaging the Powers: Discernment and Resistance in a World of Domination* (Minneapolis: Fortress Press, 1992).

81   *Ayudar a las almas*, literally, 'to help souls': Ignatius, 'Reminiscences (Autobiography)', n.54.

82   Jerónimo Nadal, *Commentarii de Instituto Societatis Iesu*, ed. Michael Nicolau, Monumenta

Historica Societatis Iesu, volume 90 (Rome: Institutum Historicum Societatis Iesu, 1962), 365.

83   John Henry Newman, *An Essay on the Development of Christian Doctrine* (Harmondsworth: Penguin, 1974), 100.

84   Newman, *An Essay on the Development of Christian Doctrine*, 100.

85   *The Jes – 150 Years of the Jesuits in Galway, 1862–2012*, edited by Tom Kenny (Galway: Colaiste Iognaid, 2014), 113.

86   An accessible book on community is M Scott Peck's *The Different Drum: The Creation of True Community – The First Step to World Peace* (London: Rider, 1987).

87   See Leonardo Boff, *Trinity and Society* (London: Burns and Oates, 1988).

88   For more on the Greek words for love, see CS Lewis, *The Four Loves* (New York: Harcourt Brace, 1960).

89   *Remembering Iñigo: Glimpses of the Life of Saint Ignatius Loyola: The* Memoriale *of Luis Gonçalves da Câmara*, translated by Alexander Eaglestone and Joseph A Munitiz (Leominster: Gracewing, 2004), n.86: 'He always inclines more towards love, indeed to such a point that everything appears as love'.

90   Raymond Carver, 'Late Fragment', in *All of Us: The Collected Poems* (London: Harvill, 1996), 294.

91   Peter-Hans Kolvenbach, at the Fifth Congress of Jesuit Alumni. Sydney, July 1997. Quoted in Charles J Healey, *Praying with the Jesuits* (New York: Paulist, 2011), 72.

92   Kolvenbach, quoted in Healey, *Praying with the Jesuits*, 72.

93   The literature on discernment is vast. Two accessible studies are: Elizabeth Liebert, *The Way of Discernment* (London: John Knox Press, 2008) and Dean Brackley, *The Call to Discernment in Troubled Times* (New York: Crossroad, 2004). My forthcoming book, *Making Good Decision* is to be published by Veritas, Dublin in 2015. It aims to provide a manageable introduction to this fascinating topic.

94   Edward Schillebeeckx, *Christ: The Experience of Jesus as Lord* (New York: Crossroad, 1980), p 19.

95   Jesuits have written innumerable versions of the Examen. Consult http://www.ignatianspirituality. com/ignatian-prayer/the-examen. For an independent, non-Jesuit perspective, try Timothy Gallagher, *The Examen Prayer: Ignatian Wisdom for Our Lives Today* (New York: Crossroad, 2006).

96   Gerard Manley Hopkins, 'That Nature is a Heraclitean Fire and of the Comfort of the Resurrection', in *Poems of Gerard Manley Hopkins*,105.

97   In Chiara Lubich, *Essential Writings: Spirituality, Dialogue, Culture* (new York: New City Press, 2007), 226.

98   Paul VI, *Evangelii nuntiandi*, n.41, available at http://www.vatican.va/holy_father/paul_vi/ apost_exhortations/documents/hf_p-vi_exh_19751208_evangelii-nuntiandi_en.html

99   Pope Francis, homily, church of the Gesù, Rome, 3 January 2014, available at http://w2.vatican. va/content/francesco/en/homilies/2014/documents/papa-francesco_20140103_omelia-santissimo-nome-gesu.pdf

100 Peter McVerry, 'The Compassionate Person', available at http://www.youtube.com/ watch?v=SKmYa7cOXvc.

101 Quoted in O'Malley, *The First Jesuits*, 209.